D1245596

IRISH
REBELLIONS

Praise for Helen Litton:

'This autobiography, edited with great skill by Helen Litton, is particularly valuable as it casts a fresh perspective on key figures and moments in the struggle for independence.' *The Irish Catholic* on *Kathleen Clarke: Revolutionary Woman*

'[A]n uncomplicated biography of the éminence grise of the Rising.' *Sunday Business Post* on *Thomas Clarke: 16 Lives*

'As a short intelligent overview of 1845–50, it will be hard to surpass.' *RTÉ Guide* on *The Irish Famine: An Illustrated History*

IRISH
REBELLIONS
1798 - 1921

HELEN LITTON

THE O'BRIEN PRESS
DUBLIN

First published 2018 by The O'Brien Press Ltd,
12 Terenure Road East, Rathgar, Dublin 6, D06 HD27, Ireland.
Tel: +353 1 4923333; Fax: +353 1 4922777
E-mail: books@obrien.ie; Website: www.obrien.ie
The O'Brien Press is a member of Publishing Ireland.

First published, in shorter form, by Wolfhound Press Ltd in 1998.

ISBN: 978-184717-969-2

10 9 8 7 6 5 4 3 2 1
23 22 21 20 19 18

Printed and bound in Poland by Białostockie Zakłady Graficzne S.A.
The paper in this book is produced using pulp from managed forests.

Published in

DUBLIN
UNESCO
City of Literature

Contents

Ruins of G.P.O., Dublin,
as seen from top of Nelson's Pillar

INTRODUCTION

ROBERT EMMET
When my country takes her place among the nations of
the earth then and not till then let my epitaph be written

From the time that Britain first began to take an interest in the country on her western flank in the twelfth century, the history of the two islands was one of constant struggle. The most important developments are often those that take place slowly and quietly, taking years to mature, but these possibilities of forward movement can be side-tracked or derailed completely by sudden eruptions of violence. Sometimes these eruptions help to encourage something which might otherwise not have happened.

The 1798 Rebellion, and those following it, were manifestations of a groundswell of movement for civil and religious rights, and national independence, in a way not true of earlier uprisings. The seventeenth-century Nine Years' War, for example, spearheaded by Hugh O'Neill, earl of Tyrone and Rory O'Donnell, earl of Tyrconnell, was a final, despairing effort to hold onto ancestral lands, and prevent the inexorable movement of Tudor power throughout Ireland. The war ended when the chiefs of Ireland sailed away to Spain in September 1607, an event known as 'The Flight of the Earls'. They left their people behind in a war-ravaged countryside, facing starvation and brutality. It is unlikely that these leaders were thinking in 'nationalistic' terms; nationalism, as such, was a development of the eighteenth and nineteenth centuries. Each chief was fighting for his own heritage, and to hold on to the old Gaelic traditions.

The Tudor system of plantations, i.e., 'planting' Protestant settlers from Britain in confiscated lands in Ireland, continued through the seventeenth century. Any whiff of rebellion merely provided the authorities with further excuses to confiscate land, a sort of fig-leaf to conceal greed. The tensions caused by placing small, vulnerable groups of foreign settlers among large numbers of resentful, disaffected natives often led to brutal and despairing outbreaks, instantly punished by the arrival of troops.

One of these was the 1641 Rebellion, planned in Ulster by members of the dispossessed noble Gaelic families. Rebels plundered Dundalk, Newry, Carrickmacross and other towns. Many settler families were killed or injured, and rumours of mass slaughters terrified the planters. The rising spread to Connacht and Leinster, and as far as Limerick and Tipperary, but by spring of 1642, it had been defeated. The Confederate War which followed lasted until 1644. The uprising rooted itself in Protestant mythology as an example of what Irish Catholics were capable of if they were not strictly controlled, or, preferably, exterminated. But there had been very little in the way of central co-ordination or national aim to begin with.

This book may help to demonstrate how successful later leaders actually were, either in imposing any kind of central command, or in developing a universally supported aim through their activities.

I am exceedingly grateful to The O'Brien Press for allowing me to make some additions to the original text, including the new chapter on the War of Independence, and for their assistance in choosing illustrations.

One:

THE REBELLION OF

1798

THE GRAND WOLFE TONE.

Drawn on Stone by J. Robinson from a Portrait by Catherine Sampson Tone.

Published March 12th 1822 by Henry Colburn London.

Printed by C. Hullmandel.

The train of explosive which led to rebellion in 1798 was laid by the American War of Independence (1775–83), and the fuse was lit by the French Revolution of 1789. Eighteenth-century Western Europe was a ferment of new ideas about the 'Rights of Man', democracy and republicanism, and a growing resentment of tyranny and royalism.

In Ireland, these ideas were slow to take root, largely because there was no system of universal education. Those who were first attracted by them were educated middle-class gentlemen, including some members of the Irish Parliament, based in Dublin. Many of those involved in the United Irish movement, which instigated the rebellion, were Presbyterians, belonging to a form of Protestantism which differed from the dominant Church of Ireland. Presbyterians had suffered along with Roman Catholics under a range of Penal Laws, which discriminated against those who were not Church of Ireland adherents.

In 1793, a Catholic Relief Act gave Catholics some legal freedoms, but not enough. New thinking about the equality of all humankind in the sight of God, and the offensiveness of bigotry and prejudice on the grounds of religion, inspired the leaders of the 1798 Rebellion to work for a freer and more equal society. This would mean removing the monarch as the head of state, and they accepted that this could be done only by force.

Roots of the United Irishmen

The Volunteers, a people's militia, had been formed in Ireland in 1778 to defend the country against possible invasion by France, while Britain was embroiled in the American War of Independence. The Volunteers gradually developed in a political direction, and supported the principle that the Irish Parliament should be fully independent of the British Parliament at Westminster. At that time, laws passed in the Irish Parliament had to be ratified in Westminster, and could be overturned there too. Some Irish MPs were growing impatient at this lack of autonomy, but others were looking for even closer links with Britain, with one parliament for both countries.

In Dungannon, County Tyrone, a huge Volunteer Convention was held in 1782; by then, the Volunteers numbered about 80,000. This movement placed intense pressure on the British government, and the Irish Parliament was allowed to pass a 'Declaration of Independence'. This gave it a larger degree of executive function, but it was still executively dependent on Britain, and any sense of freedom was more apparent than real. It was known as 'Grattan's Parliament' after its most prominent and charismatic member, Henry Grattan, and it lasted until 1800, when an Act of Union between Britain and Ireland swept it away completely.

In 1782, a Relief Act gave Catholics full rights to own land and property, and the need for resistance to British rule seemed even less urgent. The Volunteer companies gradually disbanded, unwilling to take the final step of physically attacking the institutions of the

HENRY GRATTAN.

AFTER THE PICTURE BY J. RAMSAY.

Henry Grattan (1746–1820) was educated at Trinity College, Dublin, and was called to the Bar in 1772, became an MP in the Irish Parliament in 1775, and was prominent in calling for its independence from the British Parliament. When this was achieved in 1782, it became known as 'Grattan's Parliament', although he refused to hold any office. A noted orator, he campaigned for Catholic Emancipation, and later strongly opposed the Act of Union (1800) under which the parliaments were reunited.

state, but a remnant formed a secret radical committee in Belfast, to win support for revolutionary ideas. These radicals were brought together by their admiration for a pamphlet called 'An Argument on Behalf of the Catholics of Ireland'. The anonymous author called for Protestant and Catholic to join together in mutual respect and esteem, to fight for Irish independence. Samuel Neilson, a leader of the Belfast committee, contacted the author of the pamphlet through Thomas Russell, another radical, and found him to be a young Protestant called Theobald Wolfe Tone.

Wolfe Tone was a member of the Catholic Committee, a Dublin group which worked for Catholic civil rights, but he was moving away from its fairly conservative views towards a more extreme republicanism. He is described as having 'a hatchet face, a long aquiline nose, rather handsome and genteel-looking, with lank, straight hair combed down on his sickly red cheek'. A student of law and married at twenty-two, he had not yet settled on a career.

Thomas Russell (1767–1803) was born in County Cork, served with the British Army in India, and then joined the United Irishmen in Belfast. Arrested in 1796, he was imprisoned in Scotland until 1802, missing the 1798 Rebellion. Later, having met Robert Emmet in Paris, he supported his rising of 1803, and tried to rescue Emmet from imprisonment. Betrayed, he was tried for high treason, and hanged. He was known as 'The Man from God Knows Where'.

Theobald Wolfe Tone (1763–98), the son of a Dublin coachmaker, studied at Trinity College, Dublin and was called to the Bar in 1789. He founded the Society of United Irishmen in 1791 with Thomas Russell and James 'Napper' Tandy. They wanted to break the link with England, and to institute full civil liberties for all, without religious discrimination. Wolfe Tone was threatened with a treason trial, but allowed to emigrate to the United States with his family in 1795. Hearing of the Rising in 1798, he sailed from France with a small force, but was captured and sentenced to death. He cut his own throat in prison, and was buried at Bodenstown, County Kildare.

… We have agreed to form an association, to be called 'THE SOCIETY OF UNITED IRISHMEN'. And we do pledge ourselves to our country, and mutually to each other, that we will steadily support, and endeavour, by all due means, to carry into effect, the following resolutions:

First Resolved, That the weight of English influence in the Government of this country is so great, as to require a cordial union among ALL THE PEOPLE OF IRELAND, to maintain that balance which is essential to the preservation of our liberties, and the extension of our commerce.

Second, That the constitutional mode by which this influence can be opposed, is by a complete and radical reform of the representation, of the people in Parliament.

Third, That no reform is practicable, efficacious, or just, which shall not include Irishmen of every *religious* persuasion.

Satisfied, as we are, that the internecine divisions among Irishmen have too often given encouragement and impunity to profligate, audacious, and corrupt Administrations, in measures which, but for these divisions, they durst not have attempted; we submit our resolutions to the nation, as the basis of our political faith.

THEOBALD WOLFE TONE, Belfast, October 1791

Wolfe Tone met Neilson and his group in Belfast, and they formed the Belfast Society of United Irishmen. Their first public meeting was held on 18 October 1791, and Wolfe Tone, along with an ex-Volunteer called James 'Napper' Tandy, established a branch of the United Irishmen in Dublin. This started as more of a debating society than anything else, but its debates became more and more inflammatory, and it became a secret society in 1794. Its members made an 'affirmation' instead of swearing an oath. Other founder members included Dr William Drennan; a Wexford landowner called Beauchamp Bagenal Harvey; and two brothers, Henry and John Sheares. All of these men were Protestants.

AGRARIAN STRUGGLE

In Ireland, a desperately unfair and unequal system of land ownership, which had dispossessed the majority of the Catholic population, encouraged a long tradition of 'agrarian agitation'. Public demonstrations, often followed by riots, called for equal rights of land ownership, death to landlords, fair rents, and other demands. Occasionally small, badly organised, secret societies developed, but their main aim seemed to be the assault and intimidation of undefended neighbours, people no better off than themselves.

Such a group was the Defenders, a widely-spread Catholic organisation which raided wealthy homes for weapons and money. Although Defenders took an oath to support revolutionary principles, they were also highly sectarian, often fighting viciously with equally sectarian Protestant groups such as the Peep O'Day Boys or, later, members of the Orange Order, which was founded in County Antrim in 1795. The Defenders had no centralised organisation, and were put down relatively easily by government troops, often with the utmost brutality. Large numbers of them were hanged or transported, and the United Irishmen, observing this growing anarchy, were confirmed in their belief that the whole system of society had to change.

OPPORTUNITIES

In 1793, Britain and France went to war. The French obviously had an interest in supporting an Irish rebellion, keeping the British engaged on two fronts at once, and they began to send out feelers to republican sympathisers in Ireland. Meanwhile, Wolfe Tone had been detected in treasonable activity in Dublin, and had departed for America with his wife Matilda (1769–1849). The Society of United Irishmen was suddenly banned, although all its activities had been strictly legal. In response, Samuel Neilson established a new, secret, oath-bound society, keeping the same name, but changing its objectives towards a physical-force rebellion.

The French war went badly for Britain at first. Increasingly worried about the Irish radical societies and their French contacts, the British government passed an Insurrection Act in March 1796. The Defenders, now growing in strength and becoming more organised, responded to contacts from the United Irishmen, and the two groups came together under the one oath. This combination was unlikely to work well, as the Defenders' motivation was often sectarian, while the United Irishmen stood for 'liberty, equality and fraternity', and had no sympathy with religious quarrels.

Wolfe Tone visited France in 1796, and contacted the ruling

post-revolution Directory. Plans were laid for military aid to be sent to Ireland, under General Hoche. The French had already been in contact with two members of Grattan's Parliament, Lord Edward Fitzgerald and Arthur O'Connor. These two were close to the United Irishmen, but they had not joined them. The French seem to have been given an inflated idea of Ireland's readiness for revolution, being assured that thousands of patriots would spring up to fling the British out, and were only waiting for their brave French brothers to join them. In reality, no proper level of organisation existed to ensure the success of any rebellion.

The French sent 14,000 troops in forty-three ships, setting sail in December 1796. Wolfe Tone accompanied them, in high spirits at the prospect of revolutionary action at last. Five days later, after a stormy crossing during which nine ships either sank or turned back, the fleet arrived in Bantry Bay, County Cork. That night, twenty of the ships were blown out to sea again by strong gales, and heavy snow fell. Unfortunately, one of the ships which had failed to arrive at all had carried General Hoche, so the remaining remnant of troops did not even have a commander.

The only defensive forces immediately available to the authorities in Ireland were the Galway militia, about four hundred men. These were mobilised, but found no enemy to fight. As storms and gales increased, the head of the fleet, Admiral Bouvet, ordered his ships out to sea again, fearing they would be wrecked on the shore. Those few French soldiers who had landed briefly found that the local peasantry, while welcoming, showed no sign whatsoever of enthusiastically taking arms side by side with them, but instead concentrated on looking after the Galway militia. One contemporary letter says that the Cork Irish thought that the French had been invited to Ireland by northern Protestants. This to them meant the vicious sectarianism of the Peep O'Day Boys, and they feared the French had come to drive them from their homes.

This expedition had been a complete failure, but it galvanised the United Irishmen and the Defenders. They had not really believed that the French would support them to such an extent, but here was the proof. Membership swelled daily, proper plans were laid, and weapons were collected. Firearms were always going to be scarce, so the most important weapon was the pike. Cheaply made by local blacksmiths and set on long poles, pikes were to become symbolic of the 1798 Rebellion. Another symbol was tightly cropped hair, a sign of revolutionary sympathies, and supporters were called 'croppies'.

However, problems that seemed superficially to have been solved still remained, however deeply buried, and waited to undermine the motley alliance. As Jonathan Bardon describes it:

> The Defenders ... sought wholesale land confiscation. The bourgeois leaders had in mind a government similar to the French Directory with themselves in charge – major social upheaval was not part of their agenda. The Presbyterian farmers east of the Bann [river] ... were the true democrats seeking popular parliamentary government, freedom of conscience and expression, and equality before the law.

These disparate forces would not work together for long. By the time the rebellion finally broke out in 1798, the United Irishmen consisted of a Catholic core, under Protestant leaders. They would be facing yeomanry and militia who were mostly Irish, partly Catholic, but largely strongly sectarian Protestants.

Reign of Terror

The British authorities were shocked by the French invasion attempt, and the British administration in Dublin Castle decided that a reign of terror was the only answer. Lieutenant General Gerard Lake was authorised to run this campaign, and he proclaimed martial law in Belfast in early 1797. His troops seized enormous numbers of pikes and firearms, and hundreds of prisoners were taken in Ulster. Hundreds more were flogged and terrorised by the militia, and fifty or so were executed. The United Irishmen had been more strongly organised in Ulster than elsewhere, but by the end of 1797 this was no longer the case.

In Dublin, a government spy, Thomas Reynolds, infiltrated the Leinster Directory of the United Irishmen. He passed on details of the planned rising, and the leaders were arrested in March 1798. These included Thomas Addis Emmet, a barrister; Oliver Bond, a wool merchant; and W.J. MacNeven, the only Catholic on the Executive. Lord Edward Fitzgerald, a young aristocrat who had been a British army officer, had finally joined the United Irishmen with Arthur O'Connor, and acted as their military organiser. He had renounced his title in Paris in 1792, his wide-ranging travels having convinced him of 'the brotherhood of man' and the necessity of republicanism.

Fitzgerald managed to escape arrest in March, but was badly wounded in a struggle shortly afterwards, and died in prison of septicaemia two weeks later. He had previously arranged for his three children to be entrusted to family members, supporting his young wife Pamela. His sister Lucy wrote to Thomas Paine, the highly influential author of *The Rights of Man*: 'Citizen, although he was

The seizing of Lord Edward FitzGerald for high treason. FitzGerald managed to stab one of his attackers, but was shot by Major Henry Charles Sirr, head of the Dublin police between 1798 and 1808. FitzGerald died in prison of septicaemia. Sirr later arrested both Robert Emmet and Thomas Russell.

unsuccessful in the glorious attempt of liberating his country from slavery, still he was not unworthy of the lesson you taught him'. She enclosed a portrait of her late brother.

The government decided that the only way to prevent a rebellion was to blanket the whole country with a campaign similar to that of General Lake in Ulster. The militia (most of them, it should be remembered, Irish themselves) were given free rein to terrorise the population. It is to this period that frightful tales of flogging, pitch-capping and half-hanging belong. Hundreds of people died in agony, or survived in a crippled condition. Families began to sleep in the fields for safety, terrified that theirs would be the next house to be broken into and ravaged.

Lord Lieutenant Cornwallis, writing to London, was dismissive of the Irish militia he had to lead, describing them as 'totally without discipline, contemptible before the enemy when any serious resistance is made to them, but ferocious and cruel in the extreme when any poor wretches, either with or without arms, come within their power; in short murder appears to be their pastime'. He worked hard to maintain military discipline, and afterwards often intervened on the side of the prisoner in courts martial. He became convinced of the need to remove legal discrimination against Catholics, in order to give France less fertile ground for fomenting rebellion.

Rebellion

Despite the wholesale arrest of the most prominent leaders, rebellion did break out in the south of the country in May and June 1798. The population was being driven to a pitch of despair, and the remaining leaders risked all on one throw. Since the central committee of the United Irishmen had been shattered, there was very little coordination between different areas, and communication was almost impossible. Frantic efforts were made to substitute inexperienced leaders, and develop new strategies on the spot. The two Sheares brothers, who had escaped the earlier arrests, took over command in Leinster, but were themselves arrested several weeks later.

The area most actively involved in the 1798 Rebellion was County Wexford, but events took place elsewhere also, including in counties Antrim and Down in Ulster.

UNITE AND BE FREE

Tune, 'The Green Cockade'

Ye lovers of UNION, of ev'ry degree,
No matter what Trade or Religion ye be,
The right-hand of friendship to you I'll extend,
And hope for your pardon if I should offend.

For the Rights of Man let us always be,
And Unite in the cause that will make us Free,

Till oppression and tyranny's banish'd the land,
We'll fight for our country with heart and hand.

I'm slave to no sect, and from bigotry free,
And follow what conscience still dictates to me;
All men are my brethren who'r ready to lend
Their aid to the country, and hand to a friend.

For the Rights of Man, etc.

Let the creatures of kings, and the dupes of a priest,
Bow down to a *bauble*, or worship a beast -
Shall an impious prelate, a statesman, or prince,
Set marks to our reason, or bounds to our sense?

For the Rights of Man, etc.

'Divide then and conquer' – the maxim of knaves,
Who have practis'd it long on a nation of slaves -
But the bright star of Reason will soon let them see
That *Hibernians* were made to UNITE AND BE FREE.

For the Rights of Man, etc.

Paddy's Resource, Belfast, 1795

COUNTY WEXFORD

Wexford was a prosperous county, with a large Protestant population, and a strong liberal tradition. The stirrings of republicanism appealed to the social level above the peasantry, to the farmers and artisans, merchants and teachers, and particularly to the young. Unrest had been growing in the county throughout 1797, following the French retreat, and was fuelled by a fall in grain prices, and by defeats of liberal candidates in the general election of that year. By the end of the year, sixteen Wexford parishes were said to be in a state of rebellion. Martial law was declared in April 1798, and followed by the usual round of arrests, tortures and arms searches. The North Cork militia, who were to become a byword for brutality, brought with them to Wexford an officers' Orange Lodge, adding to sectarian tensions.

The Dublin leadership had planned the outbreak of rebellion for 23 May 1798. Local units were to attack local government forces, and Dublin would be taken over by the Leinster Directory. However, the arrests of the leaders threw everything into confusion; government troops managed to hold Dublin, and local units, rising individually on 23 May, were easily defeated. By 25 May, rebellion had broken out only in counties Wicklow, Carlow, Kildare and Meath.

Showing as they rushed into Tullow street [Carlow], with that vain confidence which is commonly followed by disappointment, that the town was their own, they received so destructive a fire from the garrison, that they recoiled and endeavoured to retreat; but finding their flight intercepted, numbers took refuge in the houses, where they found a miserable exit, these being immediately fired by the soldiery. About eight houses were consumed in this conflagration, and for some days the roasted remains of unhappy men were falling down the chimneys in which they had perished.

REV. JAMES GORDON, *History of the Rebellion in Ireland in the Year 1798.* London and Dublin, 1803

The Wexford units were uncertain what to do. As they hesitated, stories reached them of brutal counter-attacks on revolutionaries in Carlow and Kildare. A Wexford leader, a Protestant farmer called Anthony Perry, was arrested and tortured, but refused to give any information. His lieutenants panicked when they heard of his arrest, and went into hiding, so the northern baronies of Wexford remained dormant.

Other Wexford leaders whose names we know include George Sparks, another Protestant farmer; Matthew Keogh, a Protestant merchant; Beauchamp Bagenal Harvey, a Protestant landlord; as well as numerous Catholic farmers and several Catholic priests. Rebellion was opposed by the local Catholic bishop and many important Catholic laymen, and the majority of Catholic priests. Loyalist Catholics and Protestants had joined the yeomanry, a civilian militia, in large numbers as the threat of rebellion had increased, and were responsible for many arrests in early May.

On 26 May, the Wexford United Irishmen began to move. Perry

The Battle of Oulart Hill (Wexford), 1798. This was one of the successful battles fought by the Wexford rebels, where they defeated the North Cork Militia. The rebels were led by Father John Murphy of Boolavogue (1753–98), who then led them to victory at Ferns, Enniscorthy and Wexford. They were heavily defeated at Arklow and Vinegar Hill. Murphy was later captured and hanged.

had finally broken under torture, and named several leaders who were immediately arrested, including Keogh and Harvey. Despite this, units proceeded as planned, their first aim being to get hold of weapons. Large houses, often the homes of landlords and magistrates, were targeted, and many of the raids were successful. Groups began to gather at landmarks such as Oulart Hill, and camps were set up.

A number of priests joined the rebels, and among them was Father John Murphy of Boolavogue. He commanded the rebels at Oulart Hill, and they fought off an attack by the North Cork militia. Encouraged by this, they marched on the town of Enniscorthy. Taking the town, they burned it down, and set up camp nearby on Vinegar Hill. The garrison in Wexford town withdrew, and this was also taken by the rebels.

By and large, the rebels were undisciplined and untrained, and success or failure depended on individual leaders. These could be either brutal or compassionate, and many had only nominal control over those they led. On Vinegar Hill, for example, about thirty-five Protestant prisoners were executed by the rebels, for no particular reason. Nor were they disciplined in battle, relying on fierce rushes to startle their opponents.

Mr Perry of Inch, a protestant gentleman, was seized on and brought a prisoner to Gorey, guarded by the North Cork Militia; one of whom, the noted sergeant, nicknamed *Tom the devil* ... cut off the hair of his head very closely, cut the sign of the cross from the front to the back, and transversely from

The Battle of Vinegar Hill, 21 June, 1798. This was the final battle of the United Irishmen's rebellion; the rebels were routed by government troops under General Lake, using cannon.

ear to ear, still closer; and probably a pitched cap not being in readiness, gun powder was mixed throughout the hair, which was then set on fire, and the shocking process repeated, until every atom of hair that remained could be easily pulled out by the roots; and still a burning candle was continually applied, until the entire was completely singed away, and the head left totally and miserably blistered!

EDWARD HAY, *Mr. Edward Hay's History of the Insurrection of the County of Wexford, a.d. 1798*. Dublin, 1842

Entering Wexford town, the rebels freed the imprisoned Harvey, and made him commander-in-chief. Keogh, also freed, was put in charge of Wexford itself. These two men now tried to put some order on the situation and to organise a force numbering about 16,000. A column of men was sent to attack the town of New Ross, and another column moved north to Bunclody. A third part of the force began to move towards Dublin, hoping to take the towns of Arklow and Gorey on the way.

In hindsight, it can be seen that the rebel successes were short-lived, and that no real overthrow of society was taking place. But real panic developed among those living through this period of horror. Protestants, convinced that it was solely a Catholic uprising and that they would be slaughtered, pleaded with priests to be baptised as Catholics, and some could be seen at mass beating their breasts with exaggerated gestures. The wearing of green emblems or garments became essential to avoid accusations of disloyalty, and many well-bred ladies used their needle-working skills to make banners for the rebel troops. Such collaboration was conveniently forgotten once the danger had passed.

The recovery of Charles Davis of Enniscorthy, a glazier, was extraordinary. After having remained four days concealed in the sink of a privy, during which time he had no other sustenance than the raw body of a cock, which had by accident alighted on the seat, he fled from this loathsome abode, but was taken at some distance from the town, brought to Vinegar-hill, shot thro' the body and one of his arms, violently struck in several parts of the head with thrusts of a pike, which, however, penetrated not into the brain, and thrown into a grave on his back, with a heap of earth and stones over him. His faithful dog, having scraped away the covering from his face, and cleansed it by licking the blood, he returned to life after an interment of twelve hours, dreaming that pikemen were proceeding to stab him, and pronouncing the name of Father Roach, by whose interposition he hoped to be released. Some superstitious persons hearing the name, and imagining the man to have been revivified by the favour of Heaven, in order that he might receive salvation from the priest, by becoming a catholic, before final departure, took him from the grave to a house, and treated him with such kind attention that he recovered, and is now living in apparently perfect health.

REV. JAMES GORDON, *History of the Rebellion in Ireland in the Year 1798*

The rebel attack on New Ross, on 5 June, lasted thirteen hours, but the rebels eventually withdrew with heavy losses. One of the worst atrocities of the rebellion then took place, when over one hundred prisoners held by the rebels were burnt to death in a barn at Scullabogue. There was no reason to kill these prisoners, many of them women and children, who had been collected from the surrounding areas. The rebels may have been incensed by accounts of some of their comrades being burnt to death while trapped in houses in New Ross. Appalled by the massacre, Harvey forbade any other deaths or 'executions', and thereby saved the lives of the prisoners held at Gorey.

The runaways, declaring that the royal army in Ross were shooting all the prisoners, and butchering the catholics who had fallen into their hands, feigned an order from Harvey for the execution of those at Scullabogue. This order, which Harvey, himself a protestant and a man of humanity, was utterly incapable of giving, Murphy is said to have resisted – but his resistance was vain. Thirty-seven were shot and piked at the half-door; and the rest, a hundred and eighty-four in number, crammed into a barn, were burned alive – the roof being fired, and straw thrown into the flames to feed the conflagration ... A few Romanists, according to some accounts fifteen in number, one of whom was Father Shallow's clerk, had been, partly by mistake or inadvertence, partly from obnoxious circumstances in the unfortunate objects, inclosed in the barn with the protestants, and by the precipitancy of the murderers shared the same fate.

REV. JAMES GORDON, *History of the Rebellion in Ireland in the Year 1798*

The rebels heading for Dublin fought and won a skirmish at Tubberneering, under the leadership of a priest, Father Roche. They captured several cannon, and deployed them at Arklow, but they were beaten off despite a vigorous assault. The forces at Bunclody won the town from the militia, but plundered the wine shops to such an extent that they could not resist the militia counter-attack. Many rebels died here.

A man by the name of George Sparrow, a butcher from Enniscorthy, chased by the people through the streets, ran up to me and clasped me around the body, imploring protection – beseeching I might save him. I instantly endeavoured as much as in my power to give him succour, and to defend him by extending my arms and body over him, while swords and pikes were pointed and brandished for his destruction; but my endeavours proving ineffectual, and rather dangerous to myself, and the unfortunate man perceiving I could not afford the protection I intended, burst from me, and while I lay prostrate in the street, occasioned by his effort to get off, he had not run many yards when he was deprived of existence.

EDWARD HAY, *Mr. Edward Hay's History of the Insurrection of the County of Wexford, a.d. 1798*

In Wexford, Harvey was deposed from his command, accused of weakness, and the position was given to Father Roche. Harvey despaired of the situation: 'God knows where the business will end, but end how it will the good men of both parties will inevitably be ruined'. It became clear that the rebels were not capable of following through on their successes, and that the strength of government forces would finally overwhelm them. Another massacre took place, at Wexford Bridge, where about one hundred Protestant prisoners were piked or shot, and thrown into the river.

The rebels, leaving Wexford, consolidated their forces at Vinegar Hill, and here the final battle took place on 21 June. The government troops, under General Lake, shattered the rebel forces with cannon fire, and stormed the summit of the hill. A large number of rebels managed to escape, but the Wexford rebellion was over. The escapers

From Boolavogue, County Wexford, Father John Murphy is seen here leading the rebel forces at Vinegar Hill, Enniscorthy, County Wexford, where they were defeated.

divided into roving bands, desperately trying to escape the yeomanry and militia which covered the countryside. Many ended up in the County Wicklow hills under the leadership of Michael Dwyer and Joseph Holt, notorious outlaws of that area. In later years, it was said that the unmarked graves of 1798 rebels could be identified by wheat sprouting from the ground, as they had carried it in their pockets for food.

MASSACRE AT WEXFORD BRIDGE

The victims were conducted in successive parcels, of from ten to twenty, with horrible solemnity – each parcel surrounded by its guard of butchers, and preceded with a black flag marked with a white cross, to the place of execution, where they were variously put to death one after another, but mostly each by four men at once, who, standing two before and two behind the victim, thrust their pikes into the body, and raising it from the ground, held it suspended, writhing with pain, while any signs of life appeared ... As an entertaining spectacle, in fact, it seems to have been regarded by a multitude of wretches, the greater part women, assembled to behold it, who rent the air with shouts of exultation on the arrival of each fresh parcel of victims at the fatal spot.

REV. JAMES GORDON, *History of the Rebellion in Ireland in the Year 1798*

In one point I think we must allow some praise to the rebels. Amid all their atrocities the chastity of the fair sex was respected. I have not been able to ascertain one instance to the contrary in the county of Wexford, though many beautiful young women were absolutely within their power ... They were everywhere accompanied by great numbers of women of their own party who, in the general dissolution of regular government, and the joy of imagined victory, were perhaps less scrupulous than at other times of their favours. The want of such an accompaniment to the royal troops may in some degree account for an opposite behaviour in them to the female peasantry, on their entering into the country at the retreat of the rebels, many of whose female relatives, promiscuously with others, suffered in respect of chastity, some also in respect of health, by their constrained acquaintance with the soldiery.

REV. JAMES GORDON, *History of the Rebellion in Ireland in the Year 1798*

THE NORTH

In Ulster, the United Irishmen had been demoralised by General Lake's campaign, and the arrest of most of the leaders. Small uprisings took place in counties Antrim and Down, but there was no coordination between them. Henry Joy McCracken, who had founded the Belfast United Irishmen with Neilson, Wolfe Tone and Thomas Russell in 1791, took over as commander-in-chief at the last minute, but his forces were defeated in an attempt to capture Antrim town.

Three days later, on 12 June, the County Down rebels began operations under the leadership of a draper, Henry Monro. A fierce battle took place at Ballinahinch, and the rebels were heavily defeated. This was the end of the Ulster rebellion, although there were a few minor skirmishes elsewhere. McCracken and Monro were later executed. It is probable that religious differences accounted for the failure of the rebellion in Ulster. News of the massacres perpetrated by rebel troops in Wexford must have reached the north before the rising began, rekindling memories of the Catholic uprising of 1641 when hundreds of Protestants had been slaughtered.

Henry Joy McCracken (1767–98) was born in Belfast, and was a founder member of the first Society of United Irishmen in that city. Arrested in 1796, he was imprisoned in Dublin, but released in time to take part in the 1798 Rebellion. He fought in a losing battle in County Antrim, but managed to hide in the mountains for some months. Trying to escape to the United States, he was arrested, tried and hanged in Belfast.

THE MEMORY OF THE DEAD

Who fears to speak of Ninety-Eight?
Who blushes at the name?
When cowards mock the patriot's fate,
Who hangs his head for shame?
He's all a knave or half a slave
Who slights his country thus,
But a true man, like you, man,
Will fill your glass with us!

We drink the mem'ry of the brave,
The faithful and the few.
Some lie far off beyond the wave,
Some sleep in Ireland, too.
All, all are gone, but still lives on
The fame of those who died.
All true men, like you, men,
Remember them with pride.

....

Then here's their memory! May it be
For us a guiding light,
To cheer our strife for liberty,
And teach us to unite;
Tho' good and ill be Ireland's still,
Though sad as theirs your fate,
And true men be you men,
Like those of Ninety-Eight!

JOHN KELLS INGRAM (1823–1907)

Aftermath

Some of the most brutal events of the 1798 Rebellion took place in the 'mopping-up' operation which followed. The yeomanry acted with 'violence and atrocity ... shot many after they had received protections, and burned houses and committed the most unpardonable acts'. Hundreds of innocent people were butchered in their homes, and the lord lieutenant, Lord Cornwallis, expressed himself horrified at the accounts he received.

> I shall mention only one act, not of what I shall call cruelty, since no pain was inflicted, but ferocity not calculated to soften the rancour of the insurgents. Some soldiers of the Ancient British regiment cut open the dead body of Father Michael Murphy, after the battle of Arklow, took out his heart, roasted the body, and oiled their boots with the grease which dripped from it!
>
> REV. JAMES GORDON, *History of the Rebellion in Ireland in the Year 1798*

While this backlash was directed at the peasants, most of the leaders of the rebellion were tried and executed through courts martial. Harvey, Keogh and Father Roche were hanged on Wexford Bridge, and their heads were impaled on pikes. Some members of the Leinster Executive were also executed, but others were granted mercy on turning king's evidence, and were exiled.

Captn. Swayne (Captain Richard Longford Swayne) pitch-capping the people of Prosperous, County Kildare. This is one of many popular prints of atrocities committed by the yeomanry during the 1798 Rebellion. Opposition prints focused on the atrocities committed by the rebels.

For the rank and file of the rebels, there was no mercy. Hundreds were sent into forced labour in Prussia, or transported to New South Wales. Badly led and armed, many of them were victims of a cause they could not have fully understood, and were carried away on a tide of violence and anarchy. The leaders were aware that most of the rebels they led were not fighting for the wider causes of nationalism or republicanism. As Thomas Addis Emmet said in his evidence: 'The object next their hearts was a redress of their grievances ... they would prefer it infinitely to a revolution and a republic'. Overall, about 2,000 loyalists and soldiers died in 1798, but the number of rebels killed, several thousand at least, remains uncertain.

Many of the leaders who later escaped or were exiled, including Samuel Neilson, William James MacNeven and Thomas O'Conor, headed to America. They created the earliest Irish community in New York, which subsequently provided support and assistance for later Irish immigrants, and continued to fight for an Ireland governed by egalitarian and republican principles.

A postscript to the 1798 Rebellion was provided by the French, who had been persuaded by Wolfe Tone to try again. Napoleon Bonaparte, now in command of the country, was unconvinced of the importance of an Irish adventure, and was intent on sending his forces to Egypt. However, three small expeditions were provided for Ireland, one led by General Humbert. The other two expeditions were delayed, but Humbert's set sail on 6 August, with arms, ammunition and about a thousand soldiers. He was accompanied by Wolfe Tone, who was convinced that the Irish, further politicised by the appalling events of the previous months, would be keen to rise again, given a little encouragement.

Humbert's force landed at Killala Bay, County Mayo, on 22 August, and he issued a proclamation headed 'Liberty, Equality, Fraternity, Union!' Thousands of locals gathered to be given weapons and uniforms, but they were not trained soldiers, and could not be disciplined. Nor did they know how to use their new weapons; Humbert himself was almost killed by a carelessly discharged rifle.

Despite these disadvantages, Humbert's French and Irish army managed to defeat General Lake at Castlebar (the skirmish is remembered as 'The Races of Castlebar'). A provisional government was set up under a local Catholic gentleman, John Moore. This situation lasted for a month, and then news came that Cornwallis himself, the lord lieutenant, was leading an army from Dublin. Attempted risings in counties Longford and Westmeath had been defeated. Cornwallis trapped Humbert at Ballinamuck, County Longford, and after a brief battle, the French surrendered honourably and were spared. The Irish were slaughtered. Killala was then attacked, and about four hundred Irish rebels were killed.

Another part of the French expedition, accompanied by Napper Tandy, had landed in County Donegal, but on hearing of the battle of Ballinamuck, it sailed away again. Meanwhile, Wolfe Tone had been captured off the Donegal coast, accompanying the third part of the French expedition. Tried in Dublin, he was sentenced to death, but succeeded in cutting his own throat in prison, dying a week later in agony at the age of just thirty-five. He had helped to change political attitudes in Ireland forever; the dream of a republic, and of separation from Britain, had intensified. Wolfe Tone's grave in Bodenstown, County Kildare, is a place of annual pilgrimage for Irish republicans. However, his ideal of complete social and religious liberty gradually faded away in memory.

WOLFE TONE'S BIRTHDAY

June 20. Today is my birthday – I am thirty-three years old. At that age Alexander had conquered the world; at that age [General] Wolfe had completed his reputation, and expired in the arms of victory. Well, it is not my fault, if I am not as great a man as Alexander or Wolfe. I have as good dispositions for glory as either of them, but I labour under two small obstacles at least – want of talents and want of opportunities; neither of which, I confess, I can help. *Allons! Nous verrons.* If I succeed here, I may make some noise in the world yet; and what is better, the cause to which I am devoted is so just, that I have not one circumstance to reproach myself with. I will endeavour to keep myself as pure as I can, as to the means; as to the end, it is sacred – the liberty and independence of my country first.

THEOBALD WOLFE TONE, *Journal*, 20 June 1796

The United Irishmen had been unrealistic in hoping to overcome entrenched sectarian attitudes, bringing together in the name of liberty people who held little but contempt for one another's religious beliefs. Most of the Catholic peasants who took part were fighting for land ownership, not for abstract republican ideals. Nor did the rebellion reach, for example, many Irish-speaking areas which might also have risen, because the leaders spread their ideas through the printed word in English only.

June 4. £200 was subscribed by the citizens, for the wives and children of the soldiers who went in pursuit of the United Irishmen at Kildare.

John Hayes, of Bilboa, committed, charged with being a United Irishman, and attempting to shoot John Lloyd, Esq., C.P. for the county.

June 6. Michael M'Swiney, charged with being a serjeant in the United Irishmen, was sentenced to 600 lashes. After having received 100 at the Main Guard, he requested to be taken down, promising to make some useful disclosures, whereupon the remainder of his sentence was remitted.

Matthew Kennedy, charged with taking arms from the house of John Evans, of Ashroe, was executed on the new bridge, and his body buried in the yard of the intended new jail.

John Moore, convicted of being a rebel captain, was hanged on the new bridge, and buried in the jail yard.

Owen Ryan, convicted of being a sworn rebel, was sentenced to receive 500 lashes, and to be sent to serve in the West Indies for life. He received 300 lashes on the new bridge.

… Persons are hourly brought in from the country, charged with aiding and abetting rebellion. The Doonas Cavalry brought in Francis McNamara, Esq., of Ardclooney, near O'Brien's Bridge, charged with holding a captain's commission in the ranks of the disaffected. Major Purdon's corps brought in twenty from Killaloe, one of whom was a Colonel M'Cormick – also a quantity of captured pike-heads. Captain Studdert's corps from Kilkishen escorted three defenders, with their pikes hung round their bodies.

June 13. Andrew Ryan, Patrick Carroll, Michael Callinan, and – Sheehy, charged with having pikes in their possession, were whipped by the drummers of the Garrison.

Daniel Hayes, to receive 800 lashes, and be transported for life.

John Collins, 100 lashes, and transportation.

James Kelly, same punishment.

Richard Kelly, 600 lashes, and transportation.

Thomas Frost, transportation for life.

William Walsh, sentenced to death, respited, and transported.

MAURICE LENIHAN, *Limerick: Its History and Antiquities, Ecclesiastical, Civil and Military, from the Earliest Ages.* Dublin, 1866; republished Cork: Mercier Press, 1992

Two:

THE REBELLION OF
1803

By 1803, the Irish political landscape had changed. Ireland and Britain had been united in 1800 by the Act of Union, partly driven by the events of 1798, and the Irish Parliament was extinguished. The Houses of Parliament in Dublin were sold to the Bank of Ireland. Executive power remained at Dublin Castle, under a lord lieutenant, but it now answered directly to London. Dublin, losing the social and political elite which the Irish Parliament had attracted to the city, entered a period of economic decline. The great houses were closed down, and the wide streets no longer echoed to the passing of noble carriages. In rural Ireland, agrarian riots and disorder continued on a local scale, but any appetite for a rebellion had died away.

Presbyterian radical thinkers had come to the conclusion that they had more to gain than to lose from the Union. They no longer suffered under legal disabilities, and could now profit from political advancement. Protestants as a whole began to be conscious of the threat of full Catholic Emancipation, in a predominantly Catholic country, and saw the Union as their only protection.

In 1799, just as the Union was being settled, word reached Dublin Castle that the Society of United Irishmen had raised its head again. Thomas Addis Emmet, one of the leaders of the 1798 Rebellion, had been imprisoned in Scotland, but a younger brother, Robert, was said to be taking up his brother's torch. Expelled from Trinity College, Dublin for his political opinions, he had maintained contact with many United Irish prisoners, and had become a member of the remnant of the Executive which still existed.

Moves were made to arrest him, but he disappeared for some time.

ROBERT EMMET

When my country takes her place among the nations of the earth then and not till then let my epitaph be written

Robert Emmet (1778–1803) was educated in Trinity College, Dublin, but was forced to leave the college when it became known his brother, Thomas Addis, was a United Irishman. The rising he planned for 1803 started prematurely, and failed almost immediately. He was arrested, tried and executed for treason.

He was in France in 1801, but Britain and France made peace in 1802, so no help was to be found there. He found a place in Parisian society, admired by, among others, the Comtesse D'Hausonville, who wrote: 'Energy, delicacy and tenderness are expressed in his melancholy features ... The modesty of his character, joined to a sort of habitual reserve, hid the working of his mind to the ordinary circumstances of life, but were any subject started which was deeply interesting to him, he appeared quite another man'.

Thomas Addis Emmet, on his release from prison, went into exile in America, but Robert did not want to leave their parents alone in Ireland, and came home. 'I find that my father and mother have left me perfectly free to make my own choice; and that they have made the sacrifice of their own wishes, and that sacrifice shows me that I must not allow myself to be carried away by personal motives', he wrote.

Subterranean United Irish activity continued. In raids in London in 1803, thirty conspirators were arrested. They were led by a former army officer, Colonel Despard, who had tried to unite English radicals with the United Irishmen in 1798. It was alleged that a new rising was being planned for London, but it seems more likely that efforts were being made to renew contacts with Irish rebels, combining a joint English–Irish uprising with French assistance. Despard and six others were tried and hanged.

In May 1803, Britain and France went to war again. Thomas Emmet was by now in France, and messages came to him from Ireland promising a high degree of preparation for rebellion.

However, the United Irish exiles in France were divided among themselves, and Thomas had little contact with the French leader, Napoleon Bonaparte. The hopeful Dublin rebels asserted that they were not relying on French aid anyway, and were confident of victory through their own resources.

PLANS FOR RISING

Robert Emmet decided to concentrate on capturing Dublin Castle, the seat of British administration in Ireland, along with a couple of other military forts in the city. Meticulous planning was involved in preparing guns and pikes, and explosives were to be used to mine the streets, an innovative idea at the time. A notable feature of this conspiracy was its absolute secrecy. The government had its suspicions, but no confirmation that anything was being planned.

Emmet's explosives were stored in several Dublin depots. On 16 July, gunpowder in a house on Patrick Street exploded accidentally, causing one fatality: 'To prevent suffocation the persons outside broke the glass and Keenan, who is since dead, cut himself so deeply by running his arm through the pane that the effusion of blood principally occasioned his death'. The authorities, alerted by this event, searched the house, but most of the weapons stored there remained hidden, and were secretly removed later.

The date of the rising was fixed for 23 July. Emmet decided not to take the risk of postponing it after the explosion, because the authorities were now suspicious and it was likely that he would soon be discovered. He expected support from the counties surrounding Dublin, as well as in Ulster, and Thomas Russell, one of the conspirators, was sent to alert the men of the north. Russell, one of the 1798 leaders, had written, 'If the people are true to themselves we have an overwhelming force, if otherwise, we fail, and our lives will be sufficient sacrifice'.

The rebellion had little chance of success, although Robert Emmet had spent £15,000 in preparations. Communications were poor, and promised forces from County Wicklow never arrived. Men did come from County Kildare, but decided that there were not enough weapons and left again. Wexfordmen waited for a signal rocket, but it was never sent up. The notion that the whole country was just waiting for Dublin to be captured by the insurgents before it rose up in force seems to have been taken largely on faith. There was little or no evidence for it.

The explosion in Patrick Street had created a shortage of explosives, and other equipment was lost or mislaid. According to Emmet: 'The person who had the management of the depot mixed, by accident, the slow matches that were prepared with what were not, and all our labour went for nothing. The fuses for the grenades he had also laid by, where he forgot them, and could not find in the crowd.' It is worth noting, despite these inefficiencies, that detailed plans had been carried through for printing a proclamation, and for elaborate laced uniforms for Emmet and his officers.

Dublin Castle was having its suspicions confirmed. Discussions held in the open had been overheard by spies, and they were aware of mysterious groups of men arriving to the city. They did not respond with any urgency, and were later criticised severely for this. On the evening of 23 July, Emmet began to assemble his force in Thomas Street, expecting 2,000 men to meet him. Eighty turned up. Nevertheless, he distributed his proclamation, and led his men onto the streets of Dublin. Here they were gradually joined by drunken revellers and bored bystanders, and the rebel army turned into a mob.

You are now called upon to show the world that you are competent to take your place among the nations; that you have a right to claim their recognisance of you as an independent country by the only satisfactory proof you can furnish of your capability of maintaining your independence – your wresting it from England with your own hands...We have now, without the loss of a man, with our means of communication untouched, brought our plans to the moment when they are ripe for execution...We therefore solemnly declare that our object is to establish a free and independent republic in Ireland. We war not against property, we war against no religious sect, we war not against past opinions or prejudices, we war against English dominion. Fully impressed with the justice of our cause, which we now put to the issue, we make our last and solemn appeal to the sword and to heaven, and as the cause of Ireland deserves to prosper, may God give us the Victory.

ROBERT EMMET, Proclamation of 1803

An eyewitness describes Emmet as entering Patrick Street with fourteen or fifteen men, and shouting to the people around, 'Turn out, my boys, now is your time for Liberty. Liberty, my boys. Turn out, Turn out'. Getting no response, he fired his pistol in the air, and decided that it would be best for him to head to the Wicklow Mountains and Michael Dwyer, the 1798 rebel-turned-outlaw. However, the mob he deserted surrounded the carriage of the lord chief justice, Lord Kilwarden, who unfortunately was passing by. Kilwarden and a companion were murdered, and Emmet was extremely distressed when he heard of this.

The great plan had failed, and Emmet went into hiding in County Wicklow. About thirty people died in Dublin during the night's rioting, but that was the beginning and end of the 1803 Rebellion.

The murder of Lord Kilwarden, one of the most serious episodes of Emmet's rising.

Outside Dublin, the only event was a minor skirmish at Maynooth, County Kildare. Ulster failed to move at all. Emmet was finally arrested on 25 August. Russell, also arrested, was among twenty-two rebels executed. A total of about 3,000 suspected rebels were imprisoned, and in December, Dwyer himself finally surrendered, with his band of outlaws.

AFTERMATH

Robert Emmet was tried for treason and sentenced to death. His rebellion would hardly be remembered now were it not for the speech from the dock which he made at the end of his trial (see pg. 64). His words echoed for the next hundred years, and kept the torch of rebellion flickering even when hopes were lowest. His legend was also enhanced by Thomas Moore's romantic poem, 'Oh! Breathe not his name'.

Oh! breathe not his name, let it sleep in the shade,

Where cold and unhonoured his relics are laid;

Sad, silent and dark be the tears that we shed,

As the night dew that falls on the grass o'er his head.

But the night dew that falls, though in silence it weeps,

Shall brighten with verdure the grave where he sleeps,

And the tear that we shed, though in secret it rolls,

Shall long keep his memory green in our souls.

THOMAS MOORE (1779–1852)

The trial of Robert Emmet, 19 September, 1803. Numerous popular prints depicted this trial, which was notable for Emmet's final speech. (See pg. 64)

Emmet was hanged and beheaded on 20 September 1803 in front of St Catherine's Church on Thomas Street, Dublin, aged just twenty-five. His sweetheart, Sarah Curran, daughter of a prominent barrister who had defended some of the men of 1798, is said to have waved to him on his way to the scaffold. Handkerchiefs were dipped in his blood, and a legend began to grow.

Although the outbreak had failed, it left the authorities very nervous, because it had been urban-based. They were used to dealing with rural unrest, but now began to worry about controlling the growing numbers of artisans in the developing towns.

I have had little time to look at the thousand difficulties which still lie between me and the completion of my wishes: that those difficulties will likewise disappear I have ardent, and, I trust, rational hopes; but if it is not to be the case, I thank God for having gifted me with a sanguine disposition. To that disposition I run from reflection; and if my hopes are without foundation – if a precipice is opening under my feet from which duty will not suffer me to run back, I am thankful for that sanguine disposition which leads me to the brink and throws me down, while my eyes are still raised to the visions of happiness that my fancy formed in the air.

ROBERT EMMET, letter to Sarah Curran

ANNE DEVLIN

A sad epilogue to the 1803 Rebellion is provided by Anne Devlin, Robert Emmet's housekeeper. Born in 1780, she was a cousin of Michael Dwyer, the Wicklow outlaw, and frequently rode to the mountains with messages from Dublin conspirators, although her family did not engage in the 1798 Rebellion. In February 1799, she helped Dwyer's sisters remove the bodies of two executed rebels from a Leitrim graveyard to Kilranelagh, County Wicklow, to lie with their comrades. The local men considered it too dangerous, but the women had two coffins made, worked through the night digging, and succeeded in their aim.

Robert Emmet, a friend of the family, moved into a house at Butterfield Lane, Rathfarnham, County Dublin, to plan his rebellion in secret. Anne acted as housekeeper, to give the impression of a family home, and became close to the conspirators, Emmet referring to her as 'one of our own'. After the failure of the rebellion, soldiers searched for Emmet at Butterfield Lane, under the name 'Mr Ellis'. Anne was tortured to give information, but refused to speak.

My father had sometime before sent over to Mr Emmet's residence a light cart to help give the appearance of business. It was freshly painted blue. This they put standing up, a rope was put over it and about my neck ... I was hauled over and the rope was thrown across the back band. They shouted again, 'Will you tell now where Mr Ellis is?'

'No, villains, I will tell you nothing about him', I said. I thought of praying and had only time to say, 'Oh, Lord, have mercy on me' when they gave a tremendous shout and pulled me up.

How long they kept me suspended I cannot say, but at last I felt a kind of consciousness of my feet again touching the ground. Their savage shouting had not ceased at this time, and I felt a hand loosening the rope on my neck.

ANNE DEVLIN, *Jail Journal*

She was brought to Kilmainham Gaol, where Emmet, meeting her briefly, urged her to save herself, but she still gave no information, despite an offer of £500. By the end of 1803, twenty-two members of her extended family were in jail. She contracted erysipelas, the result of an insanitary environment, and was left almost blind. The cave-like cell in which she was imprisoned can still be seen in

A commemorative plaque of Anne Devlin, based on a poorly-preserved miniature painting of her.

Kilmainham Gaol. She was finally released in 1806, with her father and other family members, but they had lost their farm, and her brother Jimmy had died in prison.

> After my liberation, in the latter end of 1806,
> I frequently met with some of the former state
> prisoners in the streets; they passed on without
> seeming to recognise me. But something like an
> inward agitation was visible on their countenance.
> And although I may say I was then houseless and
> friendless, I never troubled a being of them, or anyone
> else with my distress, although I held the life's thread of more than fifty of
> the most respectable of them in my hands. But the pride of acting right con-
> soled me, and I never took into account my incarceration, loss of health, the
> long and wasting confinement, and destruction of my whole family.

ANNE DEVLIN, *Jail Journal*

Anne married William Campbell, a drayman, in 1811, and had at least four children. She was always followed by the police, and anyone speaking to her risked arrest. Between 1825 and 1835 she worked as a laundress in St Patrick's Hospital, Dublin, where Robert

Emmet's father had once served as governor. Widowed in 1846, she sank into poverty, but was befriended late in life by Dr Richard Madden, who had been involved in the 1798 Rebellion. He helped her to write an account of her life, and when she died, in 1851, he erected a monument over her grave in Glasnevin Cemetery.

... My lord, you are impatient for the sacrifice. The blood you seek is not congealed by the artificial terror which surrounds your victim; it circulates warmly and unruffled through its channels, and in a little time it will cry to heaven. Be yet patient! I have but a few words more to say. My ministry is ended. I am going to my cold and silent grave; my lamp of life is nearly extinguished. I have parted from everything that was dear to me in this life for my country's cause, and abandoned another idol I adored in my heart, the object of my affections. My race is run. The grave opens to receive me, and I sink into its bosom. I am ready to die. I have not been allowed to vindicate my character. I have but one request to ask at my departure from this world. It is the charity of its silence.

Let no man write my epitaph; for as no man who knows my motives now dares vindicate them, let not prejudice or ignorance asperse them. Let them rest in obscurity and peace. Let my memory be left in oblivion and my tomb remain un-inscribed, until other times and other men can do justice to my character. When my country takes her place among the nations of the earth, then and not till then, let my epitaph be written. I have done.

ROBERT EMMET, *Speech from the Dock*

Three:

THE REBELLION OF

1848

To the historian of the United Irishmen, and the men of Ninety-Eight, belong the details of the decline of the Volunteers. Out of the embers of that institution grew the Whig Club, and that other powerful confederacy of which Theobald Wolfe Tone was the founder. These two bodies partook of the character of their parents. The Whig Club, established by Lord Charlemont, led a dilettante life and died of its own debility – the United Irishmen were deep, bold and sagacious, and but for the errors of a few leaders, would have overthrown the empire of England in their country, and established in its ruins an Irish Republic.

THOMAS MacNEVIN, *History of the Volunteers of 1782*, dedicated to William Smith O'Brien. Dublin: James Duffy & Co. Ltd., 1845

In the thirty-five years following Robert Emmet's uprising, there was an ebb and flow of popular movements such as the agitation against tithes (compulsory payments to the Church of Ireland), and Daniel O'Connell's drive for Catholic Emancipation, ending with a Catholic Relief Act in 1829. Politically, the Reform Act of 1832, widening the franchise, allowed the election of an influential group of Irish MPs to Westminster, which was to be of increasing importance as the century progressed.

Economically, while towns and industry developed further, the rural population remained in conditions of great poverty. They were utterly dependent on the potato crop, which was subject to periodic attacks of disease. Even times of economic prosperity, such as the Napoleonic Wars (ending in 1815), made little difference to people in Ireland who paid inflated rents to absentee landlords through agents and middlemen who extorted every penny they could. Nevertheless, the Irish population grew, encouraged by the vitamin-rich potato, and the 1841 census revealed that Ireland supported eight million people, double the number at the start of the nineteenth century. However, the Great Famine (1844–48) halved this population again, as hunger, disease and emigration did their worst.

THE YOUNG IRELANDERS

The year 1848 was a time of revolution in Europe, with outbreaks in Austria, Italy and France. In Britain, the Chartist movement, seeking voting rights and social change for the working population, was making the authorities nervous. Ireland, of course, was only beginning to recover from the Great Famine.

Nonetheless, a group of idealistic young men had devoted themselves to plans of revolution. These men, known collectively as the 'Young Irelanders', had supported the great Irish politician Daniel O'Connell, the first Catholic MP in Westminster, in his mass movement which sought repeal of the Act of Union. However, they ultimately moved away from the ageing O'Connell (who died in 1847), impatient with his insistence on using slow, constitutional methods to bring about change.

One of the most influential Young Irelanders was Thomas Davis, a Protestant barrister from Cork, who developed a theory of Irish nationality. 'Surely,' he wrote, 'the desire of nationality is not

Opposite: Daniel O'Connell (1775–1848). From County Kerry, O'Connell was called to the Bar in Dublin in 1798. He agreed with the principles of the United Irishmen, but abhorred the use of physical force. One of the best-known lawyers in the country, he led huge popular movements in support of Catholic Emancipation, and for Repeal of the Act of Union. He was elected MP for Clare in 1830, becoming the first Catholic to sit in the House of Commons. He fought for tithe reform and for municipal reform, and was for a while supported by the newer generation of reformers, known as the Young Irelanders. However, they broke with him on the issue of physical force. His last years were blighted by the Great Famine, and he pleaded for his starving country in the House of Commons. Travelling to Italy for medical treatment, he died in Genoa on 15 May 1847. He is buried in Glasnevin Cemetery, Dublin.

Below: Thomas Davis (1818–45). A noted poet, Davis studied in Trinity College, Dublin and was called to the Bar in 1838, but never practised. In 1842 he co-founded a nationalist newspaper, *The Nation*, which focused on Ireland's past history and its lost sense of nationality. He supported the Young Ireland movement, and O'Connell's fight for Repeal.

ungenerous, nor is it strange in the Irish (looking to their history); nor, considering the population of Ireland, and the situation of their home, is the expectation of it very wild.' In mainland Europe, ideas of nationality were being developed in countries such as Italy and Germany, and Davis was determined to assert Ireland's right to a nationality of her own, despite the Act of Union.

Well, until a spirit of Nationality had arisen in the land and spread from sea to sea, and was not only talked of, but became an abiding principle in our lives, how could we hope to have a manly book, or a manly being among us? Or, was it that the man and the feeling both arose together, like a high-tide with a storm at its back? What else but the fostering breath of Nationality could make that genius strong, which, without such sympathy and cherishing, must necessarily grow up a weakling? For sympathy, given and received, is the life and soul of genius: without such support it crawls along – a crippled abortion, when it ought to walk abroad a giant and champion of men. Until we had proved ourselves worthy of having great men among us; until we had shewed respect unto our dead, and taken the memory of our forgotten brave unto our hearts again, and bid them live there forever; until we dared to love and honour our own, as they deserved to be loved and honoured, what had we, the Irish People, a right to expect? What goodness or greatness could we presume to claim? Until all sects and parties had at least begun to hold out a helping hand to each other, and to bind their native land with one bond of labour and love, what grace could even Nature's bounty bestow on such a graceless people?

'T.W.', Introduction to *National Songs and Ballads* by Thomas Davis, dated 20 April 1846

In 1842, Davis had founded a national newspaper, *The Nation*, with Charles Gavan Duffy, an Ulster Catholic, and John Blake Dillon, a Catholic lawyer. The newspaper advocated the development of a non-sectarian cultural nationalism, and it called for Irish self-government and economic self-reliance:

> We must sink the distinctions of blood as well as sect. The Milesian, the Dane, the Norman, the Welshman, the Scotsman and the Saxon, naturalized here, must combine regardless of their blood – the Strongbownian must sit with the Ulster Scot and him whose ancestor came from Tyre or Spain must confide in and work with the Cromwellian and the Williamite ...

The Nation was filled with articles on art and history, and reams of poetry extolling ancient days and the glorious Celtic past. Its nationalism was essentially romantic, and it did not actually call for physical force rebellion, although its language was often inflammatory. It reached over 100,000 people, an enormous circulation for the time, and it was extremely useful to O'Connell's Repeal Movement for several years. Thomas Davis died in 1845.

Sir Charles Gavan Duffy (1815–1903). A journalist and founder member of Young Ireland, Charles Gavan Duffy was born in Monaghan. He co-founded *The Nation* with Thomas Davis and John Blake Dillon in 1842. A supporter of Daniel O'Connell's Repeal Association, he was tried for sedition in 1843, but released. In 1847 he co-founded the Irish Confederation, and became involved in the 1848 uprising at Ballingarry, County Tipperary. Later an MP for New Ross, County Wexford, he became disillusioned with Irish politics and emigrated to Australia, where he became governor general of Victoria and was knighted in 1873. He later settled in France, where he died.

CELTS AND SAXONS

We hate the Saxon and the Dane,

We hate the Norman men –

We cursed their greed for blood and gain,

We curse them now again.

Yet start not, Irish-born man!

If you're to Ireland true,

We heed not blood, nor creed, nor clan –

We have no curse for you.

We have no curse for you or your's

But Friendship's ready grasp,

And Faith to stand by you and your's

Unto our latest gasp –

To stand by you against all foes,

Howe'er, or whence they come,

With traitor arts, or bribes, or blows,

From England, France or Rome.

   ...

And oh! It were a gallant deed

To show before mankind,

How every race and every creed

Might be by love combined –

Might be combined, yet not forget

The fountains whence they rose,

As, filled by many a rivulet,

The stately Shannon flows.

THOMAS DAVIS, extract from 'Celts and Saxons'

When they broke with O'Connell, the Young Irelanders convinced themselves that radical action was the only answer to Ireland's problems. In 1847, as the Great Famine decimated the population, they established an Irish Confederation, and set up local 'Confederate clubs' to spread their ideas. It was a slow process in a country racked by hunger, disease and social collapse, and by the end of 1847, only twenty-three of these clubs existed.

At the same time, a 'tenant rights' movement had begun to gather force, spearheaded by James Fintan Lalor, son of a farmer who had been part of the tithe resistance movement in the 1830s. Lalor rejected the idea of Repeal as irrelevant to Ireland's dire situation, and felt that the Confederation's idea of nationalism was too idealistic and impractical. To him, the only cause that Irish people would rally around was that of the land, and land ownership. He advocated 'moral insurrection', the withholding of rents until the landlords could be brought to see reason, but this was as unreal as the ideas of the Young Irelanders. Caught up in the relentless struggle to survive, day by day, the starving peasantry were not interested in political activity.

One of Lalor's followers was John Mitchel, a Unitarian with an eloquent pen, who had written for *The Nation*. Increasingly irritated by the lack of practical plans, he broke away from both Lalor and the Irish Confederation in early 1848. Founding a newspaper provocatively called *The United Irishman*, he preached instant and violent revolution, and published articles on military tactics. The leaders of the Confederation distanced themselves from him, but he had a

'A Tipperary Eviction', from John Mitchel's *Jail Journal*. Many popular prints depicted the evictions of tenants from their homes when they could not pay their rack-renting landlords. These evictions were aided by the police, as seen here. Such scenes led to many campaigns of agrarian agitation over the nineteenth century.

John Mitchel (1815–75) as he appeared in the frontispiece of his *Jail Journal*. A journalist from Dungiven, County Derry, Mitchel came to Dublin and joined Young Ireland. He contributed to *The Nation*, and became a leading member of the Irish Confederation. The radical member James Fintan Lalor argued that nothing would happen without land agitation, and Mitchel followed him out of the Confederation. He founded his own paper, *The United Irishman*, and advocated militant activity for land rights. Tried under a new Treason-Felony Act, he was transported to Tasmania for fourteen years, but escaped to America, where he fought with the Confederacy in the Civil War. Returning to Ireland in 1874, he was elected MP for North Tipperary, but was disqualified as a convicted felon. He died shortly afterwards. His most famous work was his *Jail Journal*, first published in New York in 1854.

good deal of support among the ordinary members. The leaders were all from comfortable, well-to-do backgrounds, and they seemed to expect change to happen spontaneously. They could see no future for violent action in 1848.

REVOLUTION IN EUROPE

Meanwhile, revolutionary activity began to spread through Europe. The revolution in France was bloodless, as the king simply fled Paris, and a citizens' government took over. The Irish Confederation leaders hoped that a similar result could be achieved in Ireland, and sent Thomas Francis Meagher to Paris. Meagher, son of a Waterford merchant, was called 'Meagher of the Sword' because of an impassioned speech he had made in 1846:

> I look upon the sword as a sacred weapon. And if ... it has sometimes reddened the shroud of the oppressor, like the anointed rod of the high priest, it has, at other times, blossomed into flowers to deck the freeman's brow ... Abhor the sword and stigmatise the sword? No, my lord.

Meagher brought back from France a new flag for the Irish revolution – a green, white and orange tricolour, modelled on the French tricolour of red, white and blue. The white, explained Meagher, signified a truce between orange and green.

Alarmed by the activity in Europe, and always nervous about the

Thomas Francis Meagher (1822–67), from Mitchel's *Jail Journal*. Born in Waterford, Meagher worked as a journalist and studied law. He supported the Young Ireland movement, and was a founder member of the Irish Confederation. After the brief skirmish at Ballingarry, County Tipperary, in 1848, he was transported to Tasmania with John Mitchel. Escaping to America, he fought in the Civil War as brigadier general of a New York brigade known as 'Meagher's Brigade', distinguished for its bravery. He then entered American politics, becoming acting governor of Montana in 1865. Travelling by sea to the Northern Territory, he fell overboard and was drowned.

risk of invasion through Ireland – Britain's 'back door' – the British government sent 10,000 troops into Ireland. *The United Irishman* was banned, but *The Irish Felon* immediately took its place. Mitchel, Meagher and William Smith O'Brien, a Protestant MP for Limerick and founder member of the Irish Confederation, were arrested and tried for seditious speeches and writings. Two of the prosecutions failed, but when it came to Mitchel, who was feared as a powerful speaker, the authorities 'packed' the jury with their supporters, and he was found guilty.

Sentenced to transportation, Mitchel was sent to Australia to spend fourteen years in hard labour. Although he had been widely regarded as an extremist, this severe treatment created a wave of publicity and public sympathy for his cause. After some years in Tasmania, he escaped to America, where he spent the rest of his life, never ceasing to work for Irish independence.

Galvanised by the arrests, the Young Irelanders finally began to lay rebellion plans, collecting money and arms, although they must have realised that the people in general were in no condition to fight. They set up seventy Confederate clubs, most of them in Dublin, but the members were untrained and unarmed. Agents were sent to France and America for support, and renewed contact was made with the old Repeal Association. A new association was formed, the Irish League.

Smith O'Brien and Gavan Duffy were thinking only in terms of arming the Confederate clubs to make a display, hoping to force government to grant their demands without actually having to fight.

Yours sincerely
William S. O'Brien,

William Smith O'Brien (1803–64) was born at Dromoland Castle, County Clare, and educated in England. He was elected Tory MP for Ennis in 1828, supporting O'Connell's Catholic Association, and was interested in land reform. He joined the Repeal Association, and was highly respected by the Young Irelanders. In 1847 he joined the Irish Confederation. He was tried under the new Treason-Felony Act in 1848, with Meagher and Mitchel, and acquitted. He supported the rising in Ballingarry, County Tipperary, feeling there was no alternative, but was arrested and transported to Tasmania. Released in 1854, he visited the United States, then returned to Ireland and, innately conservative, used *The Nation* to attack militant movements such as the Irish Republican Brotherhood.

They were very unwilling to bring the issue of physical force to a head. However, Meagher was arrested again under a new Treason Felony Act, along with Gavan Duffy, Thomas D'Arcy Magee, assistant editor of *The Nation*, and several others. All except Gavan Duffy were later released on bail.

REBELLION

Martial law was declared in several counties, and a bill suspending Habeas Corpus was rushed through parliament, usually a signal that wholesale arrests were to be made. Smith O'Brien, who had been travelling around the country to estimate its readiness for revolution, returned to Dublin, risking his own arrest. Matters had to be pushed to a conclusion, and some of the Young Ireland leaders fanned out around the country seeking support.

The only positive responses were in counties Kilkenny, Limerick and Tipperary. Shattered by years of economic insecurity, the people were apathetic, or nervous, or determined to wait until the harvest had been gathered in. As Robert Kee puts it, the Young Ireland leadership were saying that they would take up arms if the people supported them, and the people were saying that they would support the Young Irelanders if they took up arms.

The one proper skirmish of the rebellion took place in Tipperary where William Smith O'Brien, with forty men carrying arms and about a hundred more armed with stones, took part in the 'Battle of Ballingarry' on 29 July 1848. Fired on by the police from a farmhouse, the rebels fled and the leaders went into hiding. Two rebels had been killed, with several police and rebels wounded, and this skirmish was later derisively referred to as the 'Battle of Widow McCormack's Cabbage Patch'. Smith O'Brien remarked bitterly, 'the people preferred to die of starvation at home, or to flee as voluntary exiles to other lands, rather than to fight for their lives and liberties', but it is difficult to imagine what else he could have expected.

'The Battle of Widow McCormack's Cabbage Patch' was the mocking term used for the abortive rising of 1848, which consisted mainly of this skirmish around a farmhouse at Farrenrory Upper, Ballingarry, County Tipperary. Two rebels were killed, and several police wounded.

Despite the temptation of reward money, none of the leaders was betrayed while in hiding. Smith O'Brien was arrested boarding a train, and other arrests were made over the following months. James Stephens, who had been active in Tipperary, escaped to France, as did Michael Doheny, a barrister who had worked with Lalor's tenant rights movement. Although some of the leaders were sentenced to death, none of these sentences was carried out.

James Stephens (1824–1901) in a postcard by the photographer J.J O'Reilly. Stephens was born in Kilkenny, and trained as an engineer. A supporter of Young Ireland and the Irish Confederation, he was wounded at Ballingarry, County Tipperary, in 1848. Moving to Paris, he was influenced by French radicals, and returned to Ireland in 1856 to found the Irish Republican Brotherhood, a secret and oath-bound group linked to the Fenians, a similar group founded by John O'Mahony in New York. He started a newspaper, *The Irish People* (1863), but it was suppressed in 1865 and various members of the IRB were arrested. Stephens went to New York, where his relations with the Fenians worsened. He was dictatorial in manner, and continually complained of lack of money and support. He also greatly exaggerated the number of IRB members in Ireland, as was later discovered. He was deposed as head centre in 1867, and moved to Paris and later Switzerland. Returning to Ireland, he lived in seclusion until his death.

Smith O'Brien, Meagher, Terence Bellew McManus and John Martin, editor of *The Irish Felon*, were transported to Tasmania. McManus and Meagher eventually escaped to America. Smith O'Brien and Martin were pardoned in 1854, and allowed home. Thomas D'Arcy Magee ended up as postmaster general of Canada, and Meagher became general of the Irish Brigade which fought with great bravery on the Union side during the American Civil War.

Opposite: The 1848 proclamation of Thomas Francis Meagher, John Blake Dillon and Michael Doheny by the lord lieutenant of Ireland, offering a reward for their capture.

AFTERMATH

The results of the 1848 Rebellion were more far-reaching than its failure might suggest. Those leaders who reached the United States had been politicised by British behaviour during the Great Famine, and kept this hatred fresh for the Irish immigrants in America and their descendants. In Paris, James Stephens and John O'Mahony maintained their anti-British fervour and continued to plot. In Ireland, Charles Gavan Duffy revived *The Nation*, and helped to lay the foundations of a tenant rights movement in the 1850s. Most of the released leaders adopted a stance of non-violence, seeking change through constitutional means.

All of these influences played a large part in the development of the next stage in Ireland's movement towards independence, nationalism and self-determination. The Young Irelanders had been excellent publicists, and their eloquent writings and speeches remained in the public domain for future generations.

John Mitchel threw his energies into writing and journalism, and accused Britain of deliberate genocide through famine in his publication of 1861, *The Last History of Ireland (Perhaps)*. Returning to Ireland late in life, he was elected MP for Tipperary in 1875 on an anti-Home Rule platform, but died shortly afterwards.

In relation to the Great Famine, which was at its worst in the year

1847-48, the abortive rebellion had a disastrous effect on the flow of charitable funds. The British were already resentful of demands for aid which seemed endless, and now the ungrateful Irish were actually biting the hand that was trying, to some extent, to feed them. Prime Minister Lord John Russell, wrote:

> We have subscribed, worked, visited, clothed, for the Irish, millions of money, years of debate, etc., etc., etc. The only return is rebellion and calumny. Let us not grant, lend, clothe, etc., any more, and see what that will do ... British people think this.

Of course, the blighting effects of British rule, bleeding Ireland dry through an intensely unbalanced system of land ownership, were not taken into account. The Irish were seen as lazy and feckless, and entirely responsible for their own miserable condition.

Four:

The Fenian
Campaigns,
1850s–1880s

J. O'DONOVAN (ROSSA)

The normal run of agrarian unrest and 'secret societies' continued at a low level of activity, and in 1858 the authorities became aware of yet another oath-taking body. One version of the oath ran as follows:

I ... swear in the presence of God, to renounce all allegiance to the Queen of England, and to take arms and fight at a moment's warning, and to make Ireland an Independent Democratic Republic, and to yield implicit obedience to the commanders and superiors of this secret society ...'

The men who were arrested as members of this group, called 'The Phoenix National and Literary Society of Skibbereen [County Cork]', pleaded guilty, and were bound over to good behaviour.

This society and others like it had resulted from the undercover activities of one man, called 'An Seabhac' (The Hawk). This was in fact James Stephens, who had fled to France in 1848 and had never ceased to preach revolution. He had studied the organisation of various international secret societies, and was now travelling around Ireland spreading his revolutionary socialist and republican principles. He found it a dispiriting experience, as all revolutionary fervour seemed to have died. He was convinced that it was important to have at least one outbreak of republican revolution in each generation, or the cause would be lost forever. However, it was clear that, to ordinary people, the land issue was far more important than nationalism.

Financial assistance from America was becoming available, as Irish immigrants improved their status and prospects. The 'Emmet Monument Association', founded in 1854, had already offered help towards a rebellion. While Stephens knew that a lot of the Irish-American 'shamrockery' was merely emotional talk, he felt that more could be made of this opportunity. He redoubled his efforts, recruiting men such as Thomas Clarke Luby. Luby had been involved with James Fintan Lalor in an abortive attempt at rebellion in 1849, consisting of an attack on a police barracks in Waterford.

In 1857, a message from America encouraged Stephens to set up a proper revolutionary organisation, with Irish-American support, and this was founded on 17 March 1858. Originally the Irish Revolutionary Brotherhood, it was to become known as the Irish Republican Brotherhood (IRB). Stephens placed himself in sole command, and indeed his administration was extremely competent, although he was later accused of keeping too much authority in his own hands.

Initially, the Dublin Castle administration confused this group with the various 'Phoenix' societies, so it was not properly identified for a long time. Its oath, drafted by Luby, called for the establishment of an independent democratic republic, and members promised 'to preserve inviolable secrecy'. It was the first completely secular secret society in Ireland, with no clerical support at all, and its leaders were of a lower social level than previous revolutionary leaders.

In order to speed up the transfer of funds, Stephens visited America in late 1858. He did not have much success collecting money, but he did leave a new grouping behind him, headed by John O'Mahony. It was called the Fenian Brotherhood, after the ancient warrior-band of Irish legend, the Fianna. Stephens moved to France, leaving Luby as his Irish agent, and sent John O'Leary to America as his representative there. He then seemed to settle down to life in Paris, without advancing plans any further.

John O'Leary (1830–1907) was born in Tipperary, and studied medicine in Trinity College, Dublin. He took part in the rising of 1848 in Ballingarry, County Tipperary, and was briefly imprisoned. He was sent to the United States to inform the Fenian leadership of events, and back in Dublin worked on the newspaper *The Irish People*, along with his sister Ellen. This was suppressed in 1865, and he was sentenced to twenty years' imprisonment for sedition. After nine years he was allowed to go to Paris, on condition of never returning to Ireland. In 1879 he met the Irish politician Charles Stewart Parnell and John Devoy, a Fenian leader, but did not support their moves for constitutional change. However, he also denounced physical force and agrarian agitation. Returning to Ireland in 1885, he became a symbol of the old nationalism of Young Ireland, and was honoured by W.B. Yeats and Douglas Hyde, members of the Irish literary and cultural revival. In 1898, he headed the committee established by the IRB to commemorate the centenary of the 1798 Rebellion, and in 1900 became the first president of Cumann na nGaedheal. He published two volumes of *Recollections* in 1896.

A financial crisis in America delayed the passage of money, and little more happened until 1861, when Terence Bellew McManus died in poverty in San Francisco. McManus, one of the Young Irelanders, had escaped imprisonment in Tasmania, and the Fenian Brotherhood proposed that his body should be brought back to Ireland for burial. Carried in triumphant procession through New York, McManus's body lay in state in St Patrick's Cathedral until it left the country.

Stephens realised that this funeral could be used to ignite nationalist fervour, but constitutional nationalists, including the remaining Young Irelanders, were not in favour of this tactic. Neither was the Catholic Church, which condemned all secret oath-bound societies. Paul Cullen, the Archbishop of Dublin, forbade a lying-in-state in the city, but a radical priest agreed to say the funeral prayers. McManus was buried in Glasnevin Cemetery, Dublin, on 10 November 1861, before a crowd estimated by the police to be 8,000. The 20,000 strong procession to the cemetery was led by members of an IRB 'front', the National Brotherhood of St Patrick. The publicity was immense.

From this time the IRB began to be referred to as 'the Fenians', and Stephens again toured the country seeking support for a rising. He founded a newspaper, *The Irish People*, which produced nationalist and republican propaganda. The organisation in America was disrupted by the American Civil War (1860–65), but by 1864 Stephens was claiming that there were 100,000 members there.

In Ireland, John Devoy of the IRB concentrated on encouraging

Irish soldiers in the British militia to take the Fenian oath. IRB groups were being drilled and trained in the use of arms. Some were arrested for illegal drilling, but by early 1865 Stephens was able to claim a membership of 85,000 in Ireland. The members were largely working-class young men from towns and cities; only about a quarter were rural labourers. Most of the meetings took place in public houses, as there was nowhere else a group could meet without attracting suspicion, and drunkenness became a severe problem when maintaining secrecy and a tight organisation.

THE BOLD FENIAN MEN

Oh see who comes over the red blossomed heather

Their green banners kissing the pure mountain air,

Head erect, eyes in front, stepping proudly together,

Sure Freedom sits throned on each proud spirit there.

While down the hills twining,

Their blessed steel shining,

Like rivers of beauty they flow from each glen;

From mountain and valley,

'Tis Liberty's rally -

Out and make way for the bold Fenian Men!

We've men from the Nore, from the Suir and the Shannon,

Let the tyrants come forth, we'll bring force against force --

Our pen is the sword and our voice is the cannon,

Rifle for rifle, and horse against horse.

We've made the false Saxon yield

Many a red battlefield:

God on our side we will triumph again;

Pay them back woe for woe,

Give them back blow for blow –

Out and make way for the bold Fenian Men!

MICHAEL SCANLAN (1836-?)

The IRB used an extremely secretive 'cell' system, and the members of one cell knew nothing of the membership of other cells. While this protected groups from infiltration, it also created intense suspicion of 'outsiders', and led to delays in getting information through and carrying out plans. Local groups were very independent of the centre, and would involve themselves in local agitations, ignoring Stephens's primary aim of secret revolutionary activity.

MOVES TOWARDS REBELLION

The authorities, despite the cell system, had spies within the Fenians, and suddenly moved to arrest the leaders in late 1865. *The Irish People* was banned, and Luby, O'Leary and Jeremiah O'Donovan Rossa, a Fenian from Cork, were arrested. Stephens remained free briefly, and sent word to America that much of the Irish organisation was still in place despite the arrests. He himself was arrested in November, along with Charles Kickham, later to become president of the Supreme Council of the IRB. The secret 'military council' had to elect a temporary head, and chose an American army officer, General Millen. Later arrests, including that of John Devoy, were made in 1866.

Following the arrests and the banning of *The Irish People*, a Ladies' Committee was established, to take the place of the arrested men.

John Devoy (1842–1928) as a young prisoner in 1866. Born in County Kildare, Devoy joined the IRB in his teens, and enlisted in the French Foreign Legion to gain military experience. He became an organiser for the IRB in 1862, and was made chief organiser in 1865 after the arrest of most of the leadership. Arrested in 1866, he was released in 1871 on condition of leaving Ireland until his fifteen years' imprisonment had expired. Moving to New York, he joined Clan na Gael (the US Fenian movement) and built up its organisation. He consistently opposed the more militant members of Clan na Gael, who wanted to plan a bombing campaign in Britain. He ran two newspapers, *The Irish Nation* and *The Gaelic American*, with the help of the young Tom Clarke. When Clarke moved back to Ireland in 1908, he kept close links with Devoy, and Devoy was instrumental in providing funds for the Easter Rising, 1916. Devoy later supported the Anglo-Irish Treaty of 1921, but during his career he was considered one of Britain's greatest enemies.

Their main aim was fundraising, but O'Leary's sister Ellen and others worked for the IRB. The secretary was Mary Jane O'Donovan Rossa, Jeremiah's wife, and the treasurer was Letitia Clarke Luby. Devoy described them later as 'the chief agents in keeping the organisation alive ... until the rising of 5 March 1867'. The women visited Fenian prisoners, and wrote reports for *The Irishman* on the conditions in which the prisoners were being kept. A Fenian Sisterhood in the United States also collected funds, and sent $200 to Ireland in 1867.

Stephens escaped from prison with the help of two prison warders who had sworn the Fenian oath. After some months in hiding in

Ellen O'Leary (1831–89), sister of John (see pg. 94). Born in Tipperary, she worked with her brother on *The Irish People* until it was suppressed in 1865. She contributed verse to this paper and others, and mortgaged her home to provide funds for the escape of James Stephens from Richmond Prison in 1865. T.W. Rolleston edited a selection of her verse, *Lays of Country, Homes and Fireside* (1891).

Jeremiah O'Donovan Rossa (1831–1915). Born in County Cork, he was reared in an Irish-speaking area, and worked distributing relief during the Great Famine. He founded the Phoenix National and Literary Societies in 1856, and in 1858 these became part of the IRB. Financial problems forced him to emigrate to the United States, but he returned in 1863 and was arrested with other IRB leaders. Sentenced to life imprisonment, he suffered difficult prison conditions, but agitation by an amnesty campaign led to his release in 1871. He travelled to New York with John Devoy, and became head centre of the Fenians in 1877. He established a fund with which to run a bombing campaign in Britain, but Devoy and Clan na Gael opposed this, and they parted in 1880. He continued to attack Britain through his paper, *United Ireland*, occasionally returning to Ireland, but he became more alienated from his former colleagues. When he died in New York, his funeral in Ireland became a massive nationalist demonstration, orchestrated by the IRB.

Dublin, he was smuggled to France, from where he hoped to reach America. He had decided that any rebellion must be postponed, although one had been promised for 1865. Apart from the disruption caused by the arrests, word had reached him that the American Fenians had suffered a split. This was partly over money, and partly ambition. Their ranks had been strengthened by men with military experience who had fought in the Civil War and many powerful personalities were contending for authority: Stephens's choice of controller, John O'Mahony, was opposed by Colonel John Roberts. Roberts wanted to attack Canada, as it represented the British Empire, at the same time as a rising in Ireland would be taking place.

Stephens, arriving in the United States, did his best to strengthen the O'Mahony wing. Meanwhile Roberts and his followers, about 3,000 men, crossed into Canada on 31 May 1866, and occupied a border village. On 2 June they won a minor battle at Ridgeway, but were later disarmed by American forces. The American authorities had left the Fenians alone until that point, but had no wish to start a war with Britain. The Fenians had no choice but to withdraw, leaving about seventy men killed or captured.

Stephens still talked about an imminent rising in Ireland, but as 1866 drew on this seemed less and less likely. Yielding to practicalities, he tried to persuade the American Fenians that it would have to be postponed yet again, saying there were only 4,000 rifles in Ireland. The American leadership accused him of cowardice, deposed him as head and passed control to Colonel Thomas J. Kelly, another Civil War veteran. They decided to go to Ireland and start the rebellion themselves, heading first to England, in January 1867. In London they laid plans for a rebellion to start in February. These leaders included John McCafferty, Ricard O'Sullivan Burke, William Halpin, Gordon Massey, Michael O'Brien of Cork, and two Frenchmen named Gustave Cluseret and Octave Fariola. They were all experienced soldiers.

Weapons had to be provided, and the plan was to seize arms and ammunition from the English military garrison at Chester Castle. All the trains would then be commandeered by force, and the arms would be rushed to the Holyhead mail boat to be sent to Ireland. Captain Massey set off for Ireland first, to begin the preparations. He was later discovered to have given evidence to the authorities, but it is not known from what date he did so.

REBELLION

Early on the appointed day, 11 February, over a thousand men began to arrive in Chester. McCafferty was suddenly informed that the authorities were aware of the plan, and with immense effort succeeded in calling off the operation. He could not prevent large numbers of Fenians being arrested. They had been betrayed by John Corydon, a supposed Fenian who had been passing information to the authorities for some time.

In Ireland, there were apparently 14,000 men ready in Dublin, and 20,000 in Cork, but shortage of weapons was the main problem. Massey concluded that a rising would have no hope of success, but the other leaders insisted on going ahead, even after the arrests in England. They picked a new date, 5 March, but were again betrayed by Corydon, who had not yet been unmasked. Some leaders were arrested, but this news came too late to reach all the areas involved. Small uprisings took place in Dublin, Drogheda, Cork, Tipperary, Clare and Limerick.

The Irish police force reacted strongly and in a disciplined manner, so small groups of police were able to disperse large forces of the rebels. At Tallaght, County Dublin (the 'Battle of Tallaght'), fourteen police under Sub-Inspector Dominic Burke succeeded in dispersing several hundred rebels. When the Riot Act was read, shots were fired by the rebels and fire was returned; two rebels died. There were small successes in County Cork, but without overall leadership the rebels could go no further. A skirmish took place in Ballyhurst, near Tipperary, but the rebels fled when soldiers returned fire. In County Limerick, Kilmallock police barracks was attacked, but the police held them off, and about 250 Fenians failed to take the barracks at Ardagh. The Irish Constabulary was later granted the appellation 'Royal' for its activities during this crisis.

As news spread of the leaders' arrests, other groups of rebels began to disperse, hoping to get home without being noticed. The main aim of the rebellion had been, after the initial assaults, to maintain a level of guerrilla warfare, but the capture of the leaders resulted in the disintegration of this plan.

In April, already too late, a ship set sail from New York with Fenian officers, rifles, cannon and ammunition, under Generals

'The Battle of Tallaght', a print from the *Penny Illustrated Paper*, 16 March 1867. This was the main event in the Fenian rising of 1867, where fourteen police under Sub-Inspector Dominic Burke managed to disperse several hundred poorly-armed rebels.

Nagle and Millen. The ship, rechristened *Erin's Hope*, was met at Sligo Bay by Ricard O'Sullivan Burke. He informed the generals that there was no hope of any response from the people of Sligo, so they sailed on looking for somewhere to land. They got as far as Waterford before provisions began to run out, and they decided to land some of the officers and return to New York.

Twenty-eight officers were landed, and all were arrested almost immediately. The police escorting them were attacked by a mob, and Corydon was stoned when he came to give evidence at their trials. The Fenians evidently had a lot of popular support and sympathy, but the people would not come out and fight with them. Their proclamation had called for a rising of the labouring classes against the aristocracy, Irish or English, throughout the British Isles, while also seeking an Irish republic.

EXTRACTS FROM FENIAN PROCLAMATION OF 1867

We aim at founding a republic based on universal suffrage, which shall secure to all the intrinsic value of their labour. The soil of Ireland at present in the possession of an oligarchy belongs to us, the Irish people, and to us it must be restored. We declare also in favour of absolute liberty of conscience, and the complete separation of Church and state ...

Republicans of the entire world, our cause is your cause ... Let your hearts be with us. As for you, workmen of England, it is not only your hearts we wish but your arms. Remember the starvation and degradation brought to your firesides by the oppression of labour. Remember the past, look well to the future, and avenge yourselves by giving liberty to your children in the coming struggle for human freedom. Herewith we proclaim the Irish Republic.

AFTERMATH: THE MANCHESTER MARTYRS

As with Emmet's rebellion of 1803, the real effectiveness of the Fenian rising of 1867 lay in its aftermath. The headquarters in England remained active, but in September Colonel Thomas J. Kelly, now chief executive of the 'Irish Republic', was arrested in Manchester, along with Captain Timothy Deasy. On 18 September the prison van carrying them was stopped by thirty armed Fenians, and when Police Sergeant Brett, inside, refused to surrender, Peter Rice fired a shot through the ventilator, killing him. The keys were seized and the prisoners escaped.

They were not recaptured, but large numbers of Irishmen in Manchester were seized for questioning. Much of the police procedure was unofficial, and the evidence they collected was questionable. Of the five men eventually charged with Sergeant Brett's murder, only four had actually been present at the event. Rice, Kelly and Deasy had escaped to the United States, and a William Allen was charged with having fired the fatal shot. The others charged were Mr Maguire, a marine on leave who had not been

'Attack on van containing Fenian prisoners, Manchester, 18th September 1867.' This attack followed on the failed Fenian rising of 1867, when an attempt was made to free two of the leaders in Manchester as they were being taken to court. When Police Sergeant Brett refused to open the prison van, a shot killed him, and the prisoners escaped.

involved at all, and three Fenians, Edward Condon, Philip Larkin and Michael O'Brien. All were found guilty of murder.

The convicted Fenians all made speeches from the dock, proclaiming their republican principles but expressing regret for the murder. Condon ended by saying, 'You will soon send us before God, and I am perfectly prepared to go. I have nothing to regret, or to retract or take back. I shall only say, "God Save Ireland"!' This phrase was echoed by them all, and became a powerful catch-cry for Irish nationalism.

Knowing nothing of the locality I rushed up what appeared to be a street, but proved to be only a blind alley with no outlet. When I started back to make my way out the crowd gave way, but a detective struck me on the head with a heavy club, and this brought me to my knees for an instant. Rising, however, again I pushed on, tearing myself loose from those who tried to grab me, until I came to a narrow bridge crossing a canal. Here, among others, there were planted in my path two big, half-drunken women, who flung themselves on me, locking their arms around my neck, as if I were their long-lost brother. I had never tackled a proposition of that kind before, and no time was allowed me to consider how to deal with it. The detectives and mob closed in, and, after being badly battered on the head, I was seized and overpowered.

Statement by EDWARD CONDON

The authorities recognised just in time that Maguire was innocent, and he was pardoned and released. But the evidence used against him was much the same as that used against the other prisoners, and his pardon cast doubt on all the convictions. Public disquiet increased, especially in Ireland. Condon, as an American citizen, was reprieved, but Allen, Larkin and O'Brien were hanged on 24 November 1867, the first Irishmen since Robert Emmet to be executed for political action.

Irish public opinion was convinced that they had been executed on false evidence, simply for being Irish nationalists. Massive protest demonstrations were held, and they began to be regarded as martyrs. The sentences after the actual rebellion had been relatively lenient, and all death sentences had been commuted to imprisonment. In contrast, the affair of the 'Manchester Martyrs' was clumsily handled.

Memorial card for the Manchester Martyrs, William Allen, Philip Larkin and Michael O'Brien.

GOD SAVE IRELAND

High upon the gallows tree swung the noble-hearted three,

    By the vengeful tyrant stricken in their bloom;

But they met him face to face, with the courage of their race,

    And they went with soul undaunted to their doom.

Chorus:

'God save Ireland', said the heroes;

    'God save Ireland', said they all.

'Whether on the scaffold high or on battlefield we die,

    O what matter when for Erin dear we fall'.

Girt around with cruel foes, still their courage proudly rose,

    For they thought of hearts that loved them far and near;

Of the millions true and brave o'er the ocean's swelling wave,

    And the friends in holy Ireland ever dear.

Climbed they up the rugged stair, rang their voices out in prayer,

    Then with England's fatal cord around them cast,

Close beside the gallows tree, they kissed like brothers lovingly,

    True to home and faith and freedom to the last.

Never till the latest day shall the memory pass away

    Of the gallant lives thus given for our land;

But on the cause must go, amid joy or weal or woe,

    Till we make our isle a nation free and grand.

T.D. SULLIVAN (1827-1914)

The Fenians were involved in one more incident before this latest outburst of republican feeling died down. Ricard O'Sullivan Burke had been sent to Clerkenwell prison on remand, and on 13 December 1867 an attempt to release him by blowing down the prison wall with explosives went wrong. The authorities had noticed unusual activity around the prison, and had changed the exercise routine. The explosion killed several bystanders and injured many more, demolishing a row of tenements.

British public opinion awoke to the fact that the IRB was dangerous, and fear of further activity spread. In London alone, more than 5,000 special constables were sworn in. Pressure was brought to bear on the government to solve the 'Irish problem', and this new public interest helped William Gladstone, leader of the Liberal Party, in the efforts to introduce Home Rule which marked his periods as prime minister.

In the preceding winter I underwent some forty days' punishment inside of three months. It had been an exceptionally cold winter, and, after taking from me portions of my clothing, I was put into the coldest cell in the prison - one that was known as the Arctic cell. Some time before I had to complain to the director about this cell being so frightfully cold that I had known the thermometer on frosty days, with a north-eastern blowing, to stand some degrees below freezing point. I got forty days' starvation and solitary confinement in that cell. Talk of hunger and cold! Many a time I was forced to chew the rags I got to clean my tinware in an effort to allay the hunger pangs.

TOM CLARKE, *Glimpses of an Irish Felon's Prison Life*. Dublin and London: Maunsel Roberts Ltd., 1992

Conditions in Ireland began to improve. The Church of Ireland was disestablished in 1869, so the tithe question disappeared, and several Land Acts did a great deal to help both tenants and agricultural labourers. Republican emotions were channelled into an amnesty campaign, begun in 1869 by John 'Amnesty' Nolan, which fought for the release of all Fenian prisoners. Those sentenced to penal servitude experienced a harsh and often brutal regime, and the amnesty campaign ultimately forced a government enquiry into prison conditions. O'Donovan Rossa, serving a life sentence, was put forward as an election candidate while still in prison, and won a by-election in Tipperary in 1870. He was released in 1871, and exiled to the United States.

In 1870 Isaac Butt MP, once president of the Amnesty Association, established the Home Government Association, which by 1873 was called the Home Rule League. It worked democratically to establish an Irish parliament which would have responsibility for its own affairs. It was not looking for an independent republic, but was supported by many IRB members despite this. The IRB was bitterly divided about this tactic, and MPs who supported Butt were later expelled from the society.

The Home Rule League provided a road to political influence for Charles Stewart Parnell, MP for Wicklow, who also became president of the Land League. This organisation, founded by Michael Davitt, fought for tenant rights, still regarded as inadequately protected. In 1882 Parnell founded the National League to push further for Home Rule, and gained the confidence of Gladstone, who was pressing the cause of Irish parliamentary independence in Westminster. However, Parnell was named in a divorce action by Captain Willie O'Shea in 1889, and the scandal not only destroyed his career, but split the Home Rule MPs.

Parnell had been backed by leading Fenians such as John O'Leary, James Stephens and John Devoy, but the organisation never lost

Charles Stewart Parnell (1846–91) from *The Weekly News*, 20 December, 1879. Born to a family of landed gentry, Parnell became an MP for Meath in 1875, and joined the 'obstructionist' Irish MPs in the Irish Parliamentary Party (IPP). He became president of the Home Rule Confederation of Great Britain and held meetings with members of the IRB and Clan na Gael where a form of co-operation was proposed, known as the New Departure. He was also president of the Land League, which had been founded in 1879 to fight for land reform. The sixty-one members of the Home Rule movement, including Parnell, were elected MPs in 1880. When the Land League was suppressed, Parnell focused on the fight for Home Rule, founding the National League. Following elections in 1885, the IPP held the balance of power in the House of Commons. Gladstone produced several Home Rule bills without success. Just as Parnell seemed at the height of his power, Captain O'Shea, another MP in his party, brought a divorce case against his wife, citing Parnell. Gladstone refused to deal with the IPP as long as Parnell remained chairman, while the Catholic hierarchy came out against him, and, finally, the IPP split. Parnell married Katharine O'Shea in June 1891, but died four months later.

CHARLES STEWART PARNELL, ESQ. M.P.

Michael Davitt (1846–1906) in a photograph taken in New York in 1880. He was born in County Mayo but his family was evicted in 1850, and moved to Lancashire. Working in a cotton factory, he lost his right arm in 1856 when it was caught in machinery. Later, he joined the IRB, and was chief arms purchaser until he was arrested in 1870. Released on ticket-of-leave (i.e., on condition of good behaviour), he met John Devoy in New York and then returned to Mayo, where he involved himself in land agitation. He founded the Land League of Mayo, and partnered Parnell in the New Departure. He suffered several terms of imprisonment, during which he studied socialism. He was elected MP in 1882, but was not allowed to sit. Elected twice more, he was declared bankrupt and could not stay an MP. He favoured the foundation of a Labour Party by Keir Hardie, but did not join it. He sat in the House of Commons between 1895 and 1899, and was a co-founder of the United Irish League, an agrarian organisation. He visited South Africa to support the Boers during the Second Boer War, and was attacked by the Catholic hierarchy for his support of non-denominational education. He died in Dublin in 1906.

sight of what it saw as the need for a physical rebellion, without which nothing could be achieved.

A new constitution, agreed with the American Fenians in 1876, stated that the IRB could not resort to physical force unless that was decided by a majority of the Irish nation (undefined), and it was to support every move to advance the cause of Irish independence. During the 1880s, an unsuccessful campaign of terror in Britain had been instigated by O'Donovan Rossa and other Fenians in America, and this had led to the imprisonment of many Fenians for dynamite offences, again treated with great severity. Among those imprisoned during this campaign was Thomas Clarke, who was to become a major figure in Ireland's fight for independence in the early twentieth century.

The parliamentary struggle for Home Rule passed to John Redmond, who became leader of the Irish MPs in Westminster in 1900. Gladstone had died in 1898; he had worked hard for Ireland, but his two Home Rule bills had been defeated. To the Irish public, on the whole, physical force rebellion seemed a thing of the past, supported by only a few die-hard Fenians, and constitutional activity was being promoted as the best way forward. But 1898 was the centenary of the United Irishmen rising, and this was celebrated widely and enthusiastically in Ireland, urged on by the IRB. The real meaning of the movement was smothered under an emotional depiction of a purely Gaelic and Catholic uprising, led by noble and self-sacrificing priests. The ideal of a non-sectarian, all-embracing liberal democracy was swept aside.

Five:

THE

EASTER RISING,

1916

By the outbreak of the First World War in 1914, the situation in Ireland had become dangerously unstable. The fight for Home Rule had finally resulted in a Home Rule Act, signed into law in 1914. It had been reluctantly agreed by the Irish Parliamentary Party led by John Redmond that Ulster counties could opt out for six years, but would then have to come under a Dublin parliament. Ulster Unionists, appalled at the idea of living in a Catholic state and determined not to break the link with Britain, made threats of instant secession. When Britain went to war, the Home Rule Act was suspended for the duration. Ireland would have to wait.

This political ferment was encouraged by the cultural movement known as the Gaelic Literary Revival. Old Irish culture, literature, music and language were attracting increased attention, and people all over the country were rediscovering their distinguished Gaelic past. A vivid sense of nationalism was being established. Prominent among the groups springing up were the Gaelic League and the Gaelic Athletic Association (GAA). Women were very active in nationalist associations, and Inghinidhe na hÉireann (Daughters of Erin) was established in October 1900 by a number of independent women. These included Maud Gonne, an Anglo-Irish political activist, and Jennie Wyse Power, a women's suffrage campaigner whose Dublin restaurant was a meeting-place for republicans. Inghinidhe na hÉireann aimed to work for Irish independence, to support Irish culture and manufactures, and to fight 'anglicisation', the spread of English influence through Irish society.

Inghinidhe na hÉireann, photographed with their founder, Maud Gonne (seated centre, behind shield). Maud Gonne (1866–1953), daughter of a British army officer, was introduced to Fenianism by John O'Leary, and was also beloved of the poet W.B. Yeats. She became involved in agrarian agitation, and was a prominent member of the Amnesty Association, working for the release of Fenian prisoners. A member of Cumann na nGaedheal, she supported a pro-Boer committee during the Boer War. She founded Inghinidhe na hÉireann in 1900, to fight the anglicisation of Irish culture. She married Major John MacBride in 1903, but when the marriage ended she settled in Paris. Returning to Ireland after the Easter Rising, 1916, and MacBride's execution, she was imprisoned during the 'German Plot' arrests. During the War of Independence she founded the Women's Defence League, and was imprisoned during the Civil War, remaining on hunger strike for twenty days before her release. She later supported her son Seán in his establishment of constitutional republican parties.

Jennie O'Toole from County Wicklow, an activist in the Ladies' Land League, married John Wyse Power, a journalist, in 1883. In 1899 she set up the Irish Farm Produce Company and opened a restaurant at 21 Henry Street, Dublin, which would later become a meeting place for the planners of the Easter Rising and the site of the signing of the Proclamation. She was one of four vice-presidents of Inghinidhe na hÉireann, and became a poor law guardian in 1903. Strong supporters of the Gaelic League, she and John were founder members of Sinn Féin. Jennie joined the Irish Volunteers' women's auxiliary, Cumann na mBan, in 1914. During the Rising, her business was burned down, and that July her daughter Marie died. Jennie joined the Irish Women's Franchise League, a militant group, and became treasurer of Sinn Féin, by then the political wing of the Irish Volunteers. She suffered many raids during the War of Independence. She was elected to Dublin Corporation in 1920 but as a supporter of the 1921 Anglo-Irish Treaty, she resigned from Cumann na mBan and was appointed to the Free State Senate in 1922. When Dublin Corporation was dissolved in 1924, Jennie was one of three commissioners who carried on its functions till 1929 and in 1934 she became a Fianna Fáil senator. She had been widowed in 1925 and when the Senate was abolished in 1936, she left public life at the age of seventy-eight.

In 1899 Arthur Griffith, a journalist who had been in the IRB, established a paper called *The United Irishman*. He did not advocate physical force rebellion; he wanted Ireland to separate peacefully from Britain and rely on her own resources, behind protective tariff barriers. A cultural organisation called Cumann na nGaedheal (League of the Gaels) was founded to promote these ideas. In Ulster at about the same time, two IRB members, Bulmer Hobson and Denis McCullough, founded a number of 'Dungannon clubs', starting in 1905. These also had a separatist agenda, and in 1907 they came together with Cumann na nGaedheal to form Sinn Féin ('Ourselves'). This party was opposed to the use of physical force, and supported the protectionist agenda.

In 1903, the centenary of Robert Emmet's rebellion was commemorated with huge parades and demonstrations. *The Freeman's Journal* stated that this centenary should encourage Irish people to 'resolve one and all to do everything possible to hasten the day when his epitaph can be written'. John O'Leary, heading the Centenary Committee, gave a short speech on the same theme, ending, 'I have nothing more to say, but I and all of you have very much to do'.

In the north, a militia called the Ulster Volunteer Force was established in January 1913. A massive number of unionists had signed a pledge to fight Home Rule, called the Solemn League and Covenant. Some of them signed in blood. The Ulster Volunteers, 100,000 strong, were to defend Ulster from any attempt to impose Home Rule, and arms were imported from Germany and distributed illegally. The British government turned a blind eye to this, unwilling

Arthur Griffith (1871–1922), an apprentice printer, was a founder-member of the Celtic Literary Society, established to study the Irish language, literature and culture, and was active in the Gaelic League and the IRB (until 1910). In 1904 he published *The Resurrection of Hungary*, which advocated a dual monarchy for Ireland. He also called for better use of Ireland's natural resources, with an aim of national self-sufficiency, and founded a paper called *Sinn Féin* which was suppressed in 1914. He joined the Irish Volunteers in 1913, but the IRB members who ran it did not trust Sinn Féin, so he was unaware of their true purpose. He did not take part in the Easter Rising, but the British called it the 'Sinn Féin Rebellion', conflating his peaceful organisation with the IRB. After the release of republican prisoners in 1917, Sinn Féin became the name of the political movement which was linked with the Irish Volunteers, now known as the Irish Republican Army. Elected Sinn Féin MPs, refusing to sit at Westminster, established the First Dáil Éireann (parliament of Ireland), with Griffith as its president. When a truce was called at the end of the War of Independence in 1921, he led the Irish delegation to London to discuss terms for a treaty. He and the other delegates signed the Anglo-Irish Treaty at the end of 1921, but after heated debates in the Dáil, Sinn Féin, under Éamon de Valera, refused to accept the terms, and Ireland moved towards civil war. Griffith died from a cerebral haemorrhage in August 1922, and was the first Irish leader to be buried as a head of state.

to provoke confrontation. In retaliation for the establishment of the UVF, and angry that the British had made no attempt to disarm them, a huge public meeting held in Dublin in November 1913 created a rival force, the Irish Volunteers. The chief of staff was Eoin MacNeill, a professor of Irish history at University College Dublin.

Within six months the Volunteers numbered 75,000, and arms had been imported for them, also from Germany. Attempts to confiscate weapons after an arms landing in Howth led to the deaths of three civilians, shot by British soldiers under pressure on Bachelor's Walk, Dublin, in July 1914, and their funerals provided a stage for nationalist demonstrations.

Are the women of Ireland as ready and willing to do their duty to their country as their Volunteer brothers? ...

We can form ambulance corps, learn first aid, make all the flags to be carried by the Volunteers, do all the embroidery that may be required, such as badges on uniforms, etc. Classes for women in first aid should be organised at once in every town where a corps of Volunteers has been formed. Trained nurses will be found almost everywhere whose services could be acquired to give lessons. Apart from the services we can render to the Volunteers, first aid should form part of every girl's training. Almost every town has its technical classes and girls have good opportunities of learning designing, drawing, etc. They will have a chance of putting their knowledge to practical use now in the making of flags for the Volunteers. To a patriotic Irishwoman could there be any work of more intense delight than that?

CAITLÍN DE BRÚN, *Irish Volunteer* magazine, 4 April 1914

Eoin MacNeill (1867–1945) of County Antrim, was vice-president of the Gaelic League, and edited a nationalist magazine, *An Claidheamh Soluis* (The Sword of Light). University College Dublin appointed him first professor of Early and Medieval Irish History in 1908. He published an article titled 'The North Began' in 1913, leading to the foundation of the Irish Volunteers, of which he became chief of staff. He supported the campaign for Home Rule and did not know that several leaders of the Volunteers were secretly members of the IRB who were planning rebellion. When Pearse told him that they had simply used his name and influence, MacNeill immediately issued a countermanding order to the Volunteers, convinced that the rebellion would be a failure. This created a lot of confusion on Easter Monday, 1916 for which he was blamed afterwards. He was later rehabilitated among republicans. He became minister for finance in Dáil Éireann in 1918, and later minister for industries. During the Civil War, he was minister for education in the Irish Free State government. He was a member of the Boundary Commission which decided the borders of Northern Ireland in 1925, but resigned in protest at its decisions.

A women's auxiliary to the Volunteers, Cumann na mBan (League of Women), was established in 1914. Its constitution called for it to assist the Volunteers, and to fundraise in order to equip them with arms. The women were trained in drilling, first aid and the care and use of weapons, but were not encouraged to use the guns they stripped and cleaned. However, some of them went on to become excellent snipers. In May 1915, Inghinidhe na hÉireann was enrolled as a branch of Cumann na mBan.

IRB Infiltration

The IRB, relatively dormant while the Home Rule movement increased in influence, still clung to the idea of a physical force rebellion. Their 1876 constitution called for them to support all movements which were advancing the cause of Irish independence, and they began to insert themselves into the Gaelic League, the GAA, Sinn Féin, the Irish Volunteers and other groups. They acted in the strictest of secrecy, and in fact, few people realised that the IRB still existed. They recruited very carefully.

The executive of the Irish Volunteers had a majority of IRB members, unsuspected by the Volunteer chief of staff, Eoin MacNeill. A co-founder of the Gaelic League, he saw Irish nationality as an ancient tradition, dating back to the Early Christian period: 'The Irish people stand singular and eminent in those times, from the fifth century onward, as the possessors of an intense national consciousness'. MacNeill did not realise that the Volunteers were being manipulated towards violent revolution, and he ultimately opposed it.

Chief among the IRB activists was Thomas Clarke, the Fenian who had spent fifteen years (1883–98) in prison in Britain for involvement in the dynamite campaign of the 1880s. This campaign had been organised by Clan na Gael, the American branch of the IRB, headed by John Devoy, and Clarke had been trained in explosives in New York. On his release, Clarke was invited to visit Limerick by an old IRB comrade and fellow-prisoner, John Daly. Daly, now the first nationalist mayor of Limerick, was to present Tom with the freedom of the city. Clarke fell in love with John's 21-year-old niece, Kathleen, and they were married in New York in 1901, where Tom had renewed his links with Clan na Gael.

Returning to Ireland in 1907 with his family, Clarke, supported and funded by Clan na Gael, built up a network of contacts, with a view to a physical force rebellion in due course. His group of adherents included Bulmer Hobson, Denis McCullough and Seán MacDiarmada, a full-time organiser for Sinn Féin.

In 1909, Bulmer Hobson and Constance Markievicz, a woman of Anglo-Irish background but strong nationalist and labour sympathies, established Fianna Éireann for boys, modelled on the Boy Scout movement in England. Many of these boys went on to take part in the Easter Rising.

Another element in the volatile political mix of the early twentieth century was that of the growing labour and trade union movement.

John Daly (1845–1916) was born in Limerick to a strongly nationalist family. Joining the IRB, he took part in the Fenian rising of 1867, and escaped to the United States, where he joined Clan na Gael, under John Devoy. As organiser for Connaught and Ulster, he swore in a young Tom Clarke to the IRB around 1879. In 1884 he was arrested in Birkenhead carrying explosives. In Portland prison he met Clarke again, and their friendship enabled them both to withstand the privations of the prison regime. After twelve years in prison, Daly was released on the grounds of poor health after a hunger strike, on condition he refrained from political activity. Returning to Limerick (where he had been elected an MP during his imprisonment), he arranged a lecture tour in the USA and raised a large sum of money for the Amnesty Association and for himself. He opened a bakery in Limerick, and was three times mayor of the city. He established a Limerick battalion of the Irish Volunteers, and saw his nephew Edward become commandant of the First Battalion. After the Easter Rising, having lost his nephew, his close friend Tom and a newer friend, Seán MacDiarmada, to execution, Daly died in June 1916, aged seventy.

127

Constance Markievicz (1868–1927), seen here in the uniform of the Irish Citizen Army, was born Constance Gore-Booth in Sligo. Studying art in Paris, she married Count Casimir Markievicz, a Polish artist, in 1900. A follower of Sinn Féin, Markievicz founded Fianna Éireann, a scouting type of organisation for boys in 1909, which instructed the boys in military training. During the Dublin Lock-Out of 1913, when hundreds of workers went on strike, she organised soup kitchens in the slums. When James Connolly, the labour leader, established an Irish Citizen Army to enable the workers to stand up to the police, she became an officer. She fought in the Easter Rising, 1916, and was court-martialled. Imprisoned for a time, she later became a Catholic. In 1918 she was the first woman to be elected to the House of Commons, but as a Sinn Féin member did not take her seat. She was minister for labour in the First Dáil. She denounced the Anglo-Irish Treaty (1921), and was imprisoned during the Civil War. She was elected a TD in 1923 and in 1927, but died shortly afterwards in poverty, as she had given all she had to the poor. Her funeral was one of the largest ever seen in Dublin.

In 1913 this had suffered a devastating setback with the defeat of a general strike in Dublin, after months of hardship. James Connolly, founder of the Irish Labour Party, set up a citizens' army to protect workers in the future – many striking workers had been viciously attacked by the Royal Irish Constabulary (RIC), and could not defend themselves. The Irish Citizen Army was founded in 1914, and one of its first organisers was the Irish playwright Seán O'Casey. Constance Markievicz became an officer of the ICA.

Preparations for a Rising

This complicated tapestry forms the background to the Easter Rising of 1916. The IRB seized on the outbreak of the First World War as an unparalleled chance to take advantage of British involvement on the continent, England's difficulty being Ireland's opportunity. They contacted German sources in the hope of receiving weapons and financial support, and Sir Roger Casement, who had served in the British consular service in Africa, was the Brotherhood's agent in this. The IRB had been, of course, receiving financial assistance from Clan na Gael for some time.

John Redmond, leader of the Irish Parliamentary Party, called on the Irish Volunteers to join the British army, to defend the rights of small nations against the ambitions of Germany, and at least 170,000 Irish Volunteers did so. The Volunteers were irretrievably split, as was Cumann na mBan. A rump of about eleven thousand remained, most of them unaware of the IRB plan to use them in a

Roger Casement (1864–1916) born in Dublin, was reared in County Antrim. As a member of the British Foreign Service, he earned his humanitarian reputation by reports on atrocities committed by European employers, brutalising native populations in the Belgian Congo and on the Amazon River. He was knighted, and retired from the service in 1913, and became interested in Irish nationalism. He joined the Gaelic League and the Irish Volunteers. He travelled to Germany, hoping to raise support for the 1916 Rising, but decided the German aid was insufficient, and hurried back to postpone the rising. He was captured as he landed in Kerry off a German U-boat, and was charged with high treason. His 'Black Diaries' were circulated to claim that he was homosexual, which was illegal at the time, and to damage his reputation. He was hanged at Pentonville in August, 1916. His body was returned to Glasnevin Cemetery, Dublin, in 1965.

forthcoming rebellion. Clarke was devastated by the destruction of what had been a promising force, but comforted himself that the remainder were truly nationalist, and would prove themselves in the future despite their low numbers.

But the Volunteers' numbers did not remain low for long. On the outbreak of war over 50,000 Irishmen had enlisted in the British Army, and many others immediately emigrated to the United States, fearing conscription. The British responded by tightening passport regulations and limiting shipping lists, leaving large numbers of mostly unemployed young men trapped in Ireland. With few outlets for their energies, the Volunteers were a tempting prospect.

The IRB now intensified its plans for insurrection. MacNeill's aides in the Irish Volunteers were Hobson and The O'Rahilly, both IRB members, but neither of these was planning a violent revolution. However, those who were also held influential positions in the Volunteers. They included Patrick Pearse, director of military organisation, Joseph Plunkett, director of military operations, and Thomas MacDonagh, director of training. The IRB had a controlling majority on the general council, but MacNeill was still completely unaware of this.

And the change that has come over the young men of the country who are volunteering! Erect, heads up in the air, the glint in the eye, and then the talent and ability that had been latent and is now being discovered! Young fellows who had been regarded as something like wastrels now changed to energetic soldiers and absorbed in the work, and taking pride that at last they can do something for their country that will count. 'Tis good to be alive in Ireland these times.

TOM CLARKE, letter to John Devoy, 14 May 1914

In May 1915, the IRB set up a Military Council to control planning for the rebellion. It consisted of Clarke, Pearse, Plunkett, MacDonagh and Eamonn Ceannt. James Connolly was included at a later stage, because he had threatened to lead his Citizen Army into rebellion on his own if no one else moved soon. The Military Council agreed on Easter 1916 as a date for the rising. Surprise was of course essential, and the planning was extremely secret, but while this tight control prevented the authorities being alerted, it also meant that when things went wrong, great confusion resulted from lack of communication.

In June 1915 the redoubtable Jeremiah O'Donovan Rossa, of the first generation of Fenians, died in America. He had asked to be buried in Ireland, and Clarke realised the importance of such a burial for propaganda purposes. A massive procession to Glasnevin Cemetery, Dublin on 1 August was crowned by a stirring oration by Patrick Pearse. He ended:

The defenders of this realm think they have pacified Ireland ... but the fools, the fools, the fools! They have left us our Fenian dead, and while Ireland holds these graves, Ireland unfree shall never be at peace.

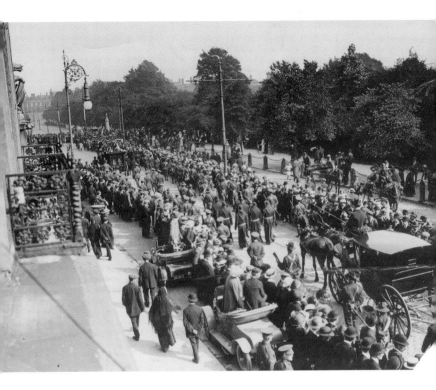

The funeral of O'Donovan Rossa in Dublin in 1915. This great set-piece event, organised by Tom Clarke and the Irish Volunteers, proved to be a propaganda triumph. The hundreds of marchers, Volunteers, Cumann na mBan and Irish Citizen Army demonstrated the strength of the republican movement, and caused many more young people to join them.

MacNeill's suspicions were being aroused. He could see no justification for a physical force rebellion without extreme provocation, such as conscription, and only then if there was a very strong possibility of success. Neither of these conditions existed, and when he was finally informed on the day before that a rising was planned for 23 April, Easter Sunday, he was appalled. He immediately published a notice in the *Sunday Independent* cancelling the nationwide 'manoeuvres' planned for that day.

This caused immense confusion among the Volunteers, who did not know whether it was authentic or not. Devastated at the possibility of missing the opportunity they had worked for, the Military Council sent couriers in all directions, altering the date to Easter Monday. These messages did not reach everyone, or were not always believed, and many local Volunteer commanders, confused and uncertain, decided to sit tight.

Meanwhile, Sir Roger Casement had suffered disaster in his attempts to land in Kerry, accompanying a shipment of German arms. The ship carrying them was scuttled by its captain, after a muddle of missed dates and a British naval threat, and Casement and his two companions, landing on the coast, were immediately arrested. When word of this reached Dublin, the conspirators realised that the rising had little hope of success. They would be hopelessly short of weapons, and Casement's arrest would have alerted the authorities that something was up. Nevertheless, they decided to go on with their plans, and make a mark on their own generation at least.

Easter Rising

The rising plans were well-laid and organised, and it might have had some chance of success if all the Volunteers had come out, if enough weapons had been available, and if the British had responded as they were expected to. However, the commandants who assembled on Easter Monday found that most of their troops had simply not turned up, and those who had were poorly armed and very short of ammunition. Moreover, James Connolly's assertion that the British would not bomb or shell Dublin's economic and financial centre proved lamentably wide of the mark.

The plotters were aided by government incompetence. Right up to the eve of the rising, sources in Dublin Castle were saying that there was no evidence of treasonable activity in the country, despite increasingly urgent messages from the secret service. It was believed that there were only a thousand or so IRB men, and that the organisation was moribund. It had been agreed to arrest prominent subversives such as Clarke and MacDiarmada, but this was postponed because the chief secretary was in London, visiting his ailing wife. On the actual day of the rising, large numbers of British officers and troops were out of the city, enjoying the bank holiday horse races, and many key buildings were very lightly defended.

On Easter Monday, 24 April, a body of Volunteers and Citizen Army, under Pearse and Connolly, took over the General Post Office in the main street, O'Connell Street (then called Sackville Street), and Pearse read a stirring proclamation to the bemused passers-by. Other commandants placed themselves in already agreed strategic positions, preparing to defend the city centre from approach in any direction. The Four Courts garrison was led by Edward Daly, Clarke's brother-in-law; Boland's Mills by Éamon de Valera; Jacob's Factory by Thomas MacDonagh; the South Dublin Union by Eamonn Ceannt, and Thomas Ashe led the Fifth Battalion, in north County Dublin. Part of the Irish Citizen Army, under Michael Mallin, took over St Stephen's Green.

As we came abreast the main entrance of the GPO, in the middle of O'Connell Street, the command rang out: 'Company halt. Left turn'. Knowing what was coming next Collins and I anticipated events a little by linking our arms in Plunkett's and moving off towards the doorway. Then Connolly's stentorian voice rang out: 'The GPO, charge!' It was well we had anticipated the movement even by seconds as otherwise Plunkett might have been swept off his feet as the party with one wild cheer made a determined rush for the doorway. The large public office was crowded with people and officials. Just as we got inside Connolly's voice again rang out in a very determined tone, 'Everyone outside'.

For a moment there was a stunned silence. It seemed for that fraction of time as if the people and officials were under the impression that the peremptory order had reference only to the members of the Citizen Army. As soon as it was realised that it referred only to the public and officials present there was a panic rush for the exits. Several officials left their counters and bolted without waiting to secure either hats or coats. The moment the public offices were closed Connolly's voice again rang out: 'Smash the windows and barricade them!'

This order was carried out with great gusto. A female voice outside rose piercingly above the din, 'Glory be to God, the divils are smashing all the lovely windows'.

W. J. BRENNAN-WHITMORE, *Dublin Burning: The Easter Rising from Behind the Barricades*. Dublin: Gill & Macmillan, 1996

Leaders of the Easter Rising, 1916. Top row, left to right, Patrick Pearse, Eamon Ceannt, The O'Rahilly; middle row, left to right, Thomas Clarke, Thomas MacDonagh (in uniform); bottom row, left to right, Thomas MacDonagh (in civilian dress), James Connolly, Seán MacDiarmada. Taken from *The Voice of Ireland* (1923), a publication by the Irish Free State government. It is not a group of executed leaders, as the O'Rahilly was not executed, nor is it a group of signatories of the Proclamation, since it omits Joseph Plunkett. It is also unusual that there are two photographs of MacDonagh.

The Proclamation Pearse read out had been signed by Clarke, Pearse, Connolly, MacDonagh, Plunkett, MacDiarmada and Ceannt, and these now declared themselves to be a provisional government at the head of a republic. But there were at most 1,000 Volunteers and 118 members of the Citizen Army engaged at this point, with at least three times this number of British soldiers and RIC ranged against them, not to mention the troops who poured into the city during the following week. The unarmed Dublin Metropolitan Police were immediately withdrawn from the streets.

About ten o'clock we suddenly noticed a well-dressed, middle-aged man coming up to O'Connell Bridge from the direction of Butt Bridge. The light of the electric arc lamps shines on his carefully-brushed tall hat. Both sides shout to him to get away. He seems dazed, and walks about uncertainly for a few minutes. Suddenly a volley rings out from D'Olier Street, and he jumps about four feet into the air. Then with another bound he reaches the corner of the bridge and rushes down Eden Quay at racing pace. There seems something unreal about the thing. Seen in the unnatural light from the street standards, one cannot imagine it to be real live drama. Involuntarily one thinks of a cinematograph show. Suddenly an officer enters the room. He orders three or four crack shots to smash the arc lamps. A few seconds later O'Connell Street is plunged in darkness. Only the stars shed a mystic glare over the house-tops.

Notes by an IRISH VOLUNTEER, *The Belvederian*, 1917

The rebel leaders were surprised at the first civilian response to the breakdown of normal life, which was confirmed by the disappearance of the police. Massive looting of city shops and pubs took place, leading to riotous behaviour. The Volunteers were also verbally attacked by local women who were married to soldiers fighting in the British Army abroad, and could not receive the 'separation allowance' while the city's administration ground to a halt.

The Easter Rising lasted for six days before the leaders surrendered, to save further loss of life. They had apparently not expected that there would be civilian casualties, but it is impossible to clear a capital city of its inhabitants overnight, particularly impoverished inner-city families with no financial resources and nowhere to go. Some of the civilian losses were the result of British soldiers shooting people in houses around the GPO and in North King Street, as they searched for rebels. A few others, including a noted pacifist, Francis Sheehy Skeffington, were executed by a British officer who was later declared insane. The full number of casualties was finally estimated at 64 rebels killed, 132 British troops and police killed, and 415 civilian deaths, which included 40 children. About 2,000 civilians were wounded. The numbers are probably incomplete, as many bodies were completely consumed in the fires which devastated the city centre after it was shelled by a gunboat on the Liffey.

Miss MacMahon came from the GPO with messages, and gave me a graphic description of what was happening there. She said, 'Mr Pearse would make you laugh; he was going around the GPO, like one in a dream, getting in the way of those trying to get things in order, and Mr Clarke said, "For God's sake will someone get that man an office and a desk, with paper and pens, and set him down to write".' There he sat writing most of the week, and brought out the paper called *The War News* ...

On Tuesday, the lovely weather continued. Early in the day, a Post Office official who was a neighbour called to tell me that he had overheard a message, sent over a private wire at the telephone exchange, to the effect that an airship was being sent over that night to drop incendiary bombs on the GPO. Could I have word sent to the GPO? Miss MacMahon arrived early with messages, and I sent her back to the GPO with the message about the airship and the bombs. The GPO was darkened that night ...

When Miss MacMahon had gone, I went into the garden to continue my planting. The ground was very dry, so I had a can of water to water in the plants. I had just laid it down when I heard a hiss, which gave me a shock. I fell over on my face and was unable to rise for some time. I did not know what the hiss was, but I examined the watering-can as soon as I was able and found two bullet-holes, one on each side. Where they came from I have never been able to find out.

KATHLEEN CLARKE, *Revolutionary Woman*

The leaders and about three hundred rebels, still holding the GPO, realised that it was about to collapse, fires having broken out in the building. Under fire from British snipers in Henry Street, they managed to reach a terrace of houses on Moore Street, but when they witnessed civilians being shot down, they agreed that further resistance was useless. On Saturday, 29 April, messages signed by Pearse were brought around to the other rebel garrisons by a Cumann na mBan nurse, Elizabeth O'Farrell, and each commandant reluctantly surrendered. Gathered in Sackville Street (now O'Connell Street), several hundred rebels, men and women, spent the night in the gardens of the Rotunda Hospital, and the following day were taken to Richmond Barracks for trial.

Although the perpetrators of the rebellion were disappointed by the outcome, they hoped that they had made the point that Ireland was a separate nation, and should be given its own place in the peace talks that would follow the end of the war. They had lit the flame of rebellion for their own generation.

In case you are anxious about my share, I had none, it was done against the leaders of the Irish Volunteers & all the sensible men among them, but there are many who will suffer innocently. Seamas [James] Connolly is a man whose chief merit is to see his country free, but he has no other qualifications for an affair of this kind. Most of the others are high-minded but utterly lacking in judgement, poets, or they wouldn't have run us into such idiocy. This is all in confidence to you. Please don't mention this opinion of mine to anyone who had no sympathy with the cause, as it is an opinion only.

FRANCES CHENEVIX TRENCH ('Cesca') to Frances Trench, 29 April, 1916

Aftermath

As with so many of Ireland's rebellions, the reaction to it had more far-reaching effects than the rebellion itself. Tried by court martial and charged with treason, fifteen leaders of the Easter Rising had been executed between 3 and 12 May, and Roger Casement was hanged on 3 August. Public sympathy had not been with the rebels to any extent, but it now began to veer around. The executions seemed cold-blooded and vengeful, not serving any practical purpose but to create martyrs.

As for the city of Dublin, devastated by that terrifying week, a Dublin Fire and Property Losses Association was formed, and about sixty claims were made by shop owners and businesses whose premises had been destroyed. Much of the subsequent rebuilding took in modern improvements in fire protection, and added steel joists for better stability. The GPO had recently been reopened after a massive refurbishment, but now lay in ruins. Rebuilt once more, it was formally reopened by the Irish Free State in 1929.

An interesting development in the subsequent treatment of the leaders, as they came to be seen as Ireland's heroes, is the extent to which the Catholic Church claimed them as its own. As Roy Foster puts it, their final letters and statements 'tapped into the long tradition of speeches from the dock enshrining national martyrology, endorsed by Catholic traditions of holy dying and sacrificial blood'. Many of them had indeed been practising Catholics, but men such as James Connolly and Thomas Clarke were not. Clarke told his wife

Top: Ruins of the General Post Office (GPO) as seen from the top of Nelson's Pillar, 1916.

Below: Interior of the Royal College of Surgeons in the aftermath of the 1916 Rising.

before his execution that he had sent a priest away, refusing to confess that the rising had been a sin. Connolly was said to have received Communion before his death, and one of the priests in Kilmainham Gaol later claimed that Clarke did also. Clarke had been excommunicated in the 1880s by the Church for being a Fenian.

Most of the rebel troops were interned in England. By the time they were all released, in 1917, they had received proper military training and discipline, and had been bound more closely to the Irish Volunteers, soon to become the Irish Republican Army (IRA). Irish republicanism now operated under the banner of Sinn Féin, as the British had mistakenly interpreted the rebellion as being controlled by Sinn Féin. Arthur Griffith and other Sinn Féin members began to make political moves towards independence, but simultaneously, the IRA started a guerrilla war which was to become known as the War of Independence (1919–1921).

I assume I am speaking to Englishmen who value their own freedom, and who profess to be fighting for the freedom of Belgium and Serbia. Believe that we too love freedom and desire it. To us it is more desirable than anything else in the world. If you strike us down now we shall rise again and renew the fight. You cannot conquer Ireland; you cannot extinguish the Irish passion for freedom; if our deed has not been sufficient to win freedom then our children will win it by a better deed.

PATRICK PEARSE, speech at his court martial

Six:

The War of
Independence,
1919–1921

By the end of 1917, most of the Irish Volunteers interned in Britain had been released, and made their way home. In stark contrast to the abuse hurled at them as they were marched away after their surrender in 1916, they now found themselves greeted by cheering crowds. Constance Markievicz, whose death sentence had been commuted to internment, was released in June, and driven in procession through Dublin streets, escorted by brass bands and trade union banners. The public mood had altered completely, largely as a consequence of the long-drawn-out executions, described by one commentator as like watching 'a stream of blood dripping from under a closed door'.

The internment of so many trained soldiers, side by side, with many who had not taken part in the rising, or had not committed

Return of Constance Markievicz in 1917 to Dublin after her internment in Aylesbury Prison, England.

themselves fully before, served the purposes of the IRB. They had bonded together as a militia, and history classes in the camps had reminded them all of what they were fighting for.

Kathleen Clarke, widow of the executed leader Tom, first signatory of the Proclamation, had been left money by him to help dependants after the rising. The Irish Volunteers' Dependants' Fund (IVDF), run by Cumann na mBan, helped the many wives and children who had suddenly found themselves without a breadwinner. Mrs Clarke had been entrusted with the secrets of the IRB before the rising in order to revive it afterwards, in the event of failure, so the fund also served as a cloak for IRB activities.

As secretary of the fund, she chose Michael Collins, a young Volunteer who had fought in the GPO and was one of Joseph Plunkett's aides. In Frongoch internment camp, in Wales, he was known for his physical horseplay and aggression in debate, but had also been a most efficient camp secretary, helping to organise resistance to the camp administration. Kathleen Clarke said he reminded her of Seán MacDiarmada, whom she had greatly admired, and he used the post of IVDF secretary to travel the country, pulling together the strands of the pre-rising IRB.

In British eyes, the Easter Rising had been planned and controlled by Sinn Féin, Arthur Griffith's strictly political and non-violent party. Bowing to the inevitable, Griffith allowed the name to be taken over, and from 1917, Sinn Féin – led by Griffith and Éamon de Valera, the only 1916 commandant not executed – developed into a nationalist political party with control over the Irish Volunteers.

Sixty members of Cumann na mBan, the ICA and the Clan na nGaedheal Girl Scouts who took part in the Easter Rising, photographed during the summer of 1916. Seated in the front row, on the right, is Dr Kathleen Lynn who opened the first children's hospital in Ireland in 1919. From 1937 St Ultan's Children's Hospital was the centre for BCG vaccination in Ireland. Also here is Rosie Hackett, back row, fifth from the right, who had founded the Irish Women Workers' Union in 1911 at the age of 18. She fought beside Constance Markievicz at Stephen's Green during the Rising and, with her background in printing, helped print the Proclamation of the Irish Republic read out by Patrick Pearse. Rosie Hackett also helped Dr Lynn in her surgery at Liberty Hall.

Kathleen Clarke (1878–1972), seen here in mourning attire, was born in Limerick, to the strongly nationalist Daly family. Her uncle John (see pg. 127) was a very close friend of Tom Clarke, whom Kathleen married in New York in 1901. They had three sons. Tom, working for Clan na Gael, returned to galvanise nationalism in Ireland in 1908. He set up two tobacconist shops in Dublin, and these became centres of revolutionary activity. Kathleen was a founder member of Cumann na mBan. She stayed home during the Easter Rising, as she had been left with money and information to help the cause if the rising failed. She was brought to Kilmainham to say goodbye to Tom the night of his execution, and the following night returned to say goodbye to her brother Edward, also executed. She suffered a miscarriage shortly afterwards. Kathleen founded the Irish Volunteers Dependants' Fund. Arrested for the 'German Plot' in 1918, she was imprisoned for about a year in Holloway, London, with Maud Gonne and Constance Markievicz. She became a Dublin councillor, and a TD, and voted against the Anglo-Irish Treaty in 1921. She was a founder member of Fianna Fáil and later became a senator. In 1939 she became the first woman lord mayor of Dublin. She retired from politics a few years later, and lived in Liverpool with her youngest son. She died there, and was brought back to Dublin for a state funeral.

At the same time, the Irish Volunteers were becoming known as the Irish Republican Army (IRA). However, the IRA was still being controlled behind the scenes by the rejuvenated IRB and Michael Collins.

Sinn Féin began its wider political moves by contesting a series of by-elections in 1917 and 1918. They won in Roscommon and in South Longford in May 1917. In June, many prisoners were released from internment and came home to general jubilation. In July, the by-election in Clare East was comfortably won by Éamon de Valera, and William Cosgrave won in Kilkenny City. 'Sinn Féin clubs' sprang up around the country.

Many members of the IRA and Sinn Féin were arrested that summer, for such activities as illegal drilling or making seditious speeches. One of those arrested was Thomas Ashe, a gentle and poetic man and leader of the Fifth Battalion during the rising, who joined a hunger strike in Mountjoy Jail, seeking to be treated as a political prisoner rather than a criminal. The hunger strikers were (as in the case of suffragettes in Britain) force fed. In Ashe's case, something went horribly wrong, and he died in hospital some days later. The strikers' demands were immediately granted, and Ashe's funeral on 30 September provoked a massive demonstration. Collins spoke briefly at the graveside, saying only, 'The volley [of shots] just fired is the only speech it would be proper to make above the grave of a dead Fenian'. Sinn Féin's membership numbers grew even more rapidly.

There was a crisis over conscription in 1918, as the First World War was draining Britain of its male population, and the need for fresh soldiers grew intense. Sinn Féin, with the backing of the Catholic hierarchy, vowed that the Volunteers would resist conscription in Ireland by force, and the authorities backed down. The old Irish Parliamentary Party was being more and more overshadowed by Sinn Féin, which was clearly becoming the voice of the people.

In May 1918, the British authorities proclaimed the existence of a 'German Plot', and many leading IRB activists were arrested. Collins, warned by his matchless information network, escaped, but de Valera was among those arrested. Kathleen Clarke ignored Collins's warning to leave Dublin, and ultimately spent nine months in Holloway Women's Prison in London, along with Maud Gonne, who had not been involved in the rising, and Constance Markievicz.

In the general election of December 1918, Sinn Féin won 73 of the 105 seats contested. Their abstention policy meant that they

An early meeting of Dáil Éireann in the Mansion House, Dublin, possibly August 1921.

refused to sit in the House of Commons in Westminster. Instead, they established the First Dáil Éireann (parliament of Ireland). Many of its members were either in prison or on the run, so the Dáil could meet only rarely, but it held its first meeting on 21 January 1919. De Valera was declared president, although he was still in prison. A Declaration of Independence was read, and a Democratic Programme was proclaimed, based to a large extent on the 1916 Proclamation. The Democratic Programme promised, among other things, to provide for all children, to abolish the degrading poor law system, to promote the use of Ireland's natural resources, to encourage industrialisation and to improve working conditions.

Collins arranged for de Valera's escape from Lincoln Jail. Returning to Ireland in February 1919, de Valera then set off to the United

Left to right: Harry Boland, Michael Collins and Éamon de Valera. The joviality between the men shows the closeness of their relationships at the time.

States for eighteen months, with his close friend Harry Boland. This was intended as a fundraising trip, and was also a propaganda event, but it did not achieve recognition for the Irish Republic, one of its aims, or gain much Irish-American support for the idea. President Woodrow Wilson was embarrassed by the visit, because he did not want to be dragged into the politics between Britain and Ireland. Irish-American groups were divided among themselves, and there were tensions between rival factions of Clan na Gael.

In 1919, both Sinn Féin and the IRA were banned by the British authorities. Meanwhile, a small guerrilla war had gradually been

Sinn Féin Ard Fheis. Seated front row, left to right: Kathleen Clarke, Eamonn Duggan, Dr Kathleen Lynn, Arthur Griffith, Éamon de Valera, Michael Collins, Harry Boland, Hanna Sheehy Skeffington. Jennie Wyse Power stands in the middle row, extreme left.

escalating. The official start of the War of Independence is dated to an IRA ambush of a group of RIC, at Soloheadbeg, County Tipperary, on 21 January 1919, the day of the first meeting of the Dáil. Two RIC members were killed. As the war progressed, the IRA, controlled by the IRB, made most of the executive decisions, and the politicians were marginalised. De Valera's absence in America for most of the war, although it raised his profile as an international celebrity, meant that he had little control over the tactics of the war, and Collins ran the show until de Valera's return in December 1920.

COURSE OF THE WAR

The War of Independence took place largely in Dublin and the province of Munster, and IRA victories were initially few and far between. Arms and supplies were a problem, and communications were difficult. Many of the fighters were new, untrained recruits. However, they were supported by local communities. Cumann na mBan played a leading role in activities, acting as couriers, providing safe houses, painting slogans on walls at night, smuggling weapons from place to place – women were less likely to be searched at checkpoints.

1. Speak Irish if you know it well.

2. Refuse to recognise the court.

3. Give no bail.

4. Demand the rights of political prisoners.

a) Insist on wearing your own clothes. Prisoners are entitled to this, and should be searched only by one officer appointed for the purpose.

b) See that you get rights in regard to parcels, letters, visits, intercourse. Every untried prisoner is entitled to write and receive one letter per day.

c) If you cannot eat prison food, refuse it.

d) Refuse to see prisoners through cage.

e) Refuse to do menial work.

Instructions to Cumann na mBan members if arrested, 1919.

There were few pitched battles in this 'war'; skirmishes consisted of ambushes by IRA 'flying columns', groups of men who moved rapidly around the countryside. However, these ambushes often led to brutal reprisals by British forces, punishing the local population by burning and destroying property and brutalising innocent victims.

The most vicious outbursts were at the hands of hastily-recruited 'auxiliary' police forces. These were largely ex-servicemen from the First World War, hardened by war themselves and disinclined to mercy. The 'Black and Tans', as they were known for their mismatched uniforms, and the 'Auxiliaries', ex-army officers, were attached to the RIC. However, they were tough and undisciplined, and stories spread widely about their uncontrolled violence and the terror they left behind them. Correspondents wrote of wrecked creameries, streets of looted and burned shops, public floggings of suspected rebels, and the random shooting of innocent civilians. This indiscipline had a predictable effect on the British military, who also began to react brutally to IRA activities.

Up to November 1920, I had 'dismissed' or 'dispensed with the services of' over fifty Auxiliary police (ex-officers) for various acts of indiscipline, but shortly after that date a heavy and hidden hand came down. My powers of dismissal and dispensal were taken away from me. Why? I had to wait a few months to find out. 'They' feared a 'kick-back' from England caused by 'talk' on the part of the 'kicked out'. Later 'they' got the 'kick' in return.

BRIGADIER-GENERAL F.P. CROZIER, commander of Auxiliary Division, RIC

The Black-and-Tans usually lived in the barracks with the RIC. Promotion among both sections was rapid; every constable could hope to be a district inspector and every sergeant a chief inspector, provided he showed his loyalty to England and his willingness to kill, maim and torture. After a while the worst of the two lots were indistinguishable, except that the old RIC knew who we were as a rule and took a good deal of pleasure in being insolent. The Auxies were supposed to be officers and gentlemen and as such were welcomed by the friends of the old garrison, but they were not accepted by high society and thought themselves insulted by the discrimination ...

GERALDINE PLUNKETT DILLON, *All in the Blood: A Memoir of the Plunkett Family, the 1916 Rising and the War of Independence*

The British authorities had reacted with confusion to the Sinn Féin election victories of 1918 and the establishment of the First Dáil. Lloyd George and the rest of the cabinet saw the Dáil as a 'stage play', and when the chief secretary asked what he should do in response, Deputy Prime Minister Andrew Bonar Law told him he could do what he liked. Lord Lieutenant French, a tough ex-soldier, believed the country was utterly unfit for Home Rule. He wanted an extension of military powers, and the suppression of Sinn Féin and Dáil Éireann, but putting the country under martial law was not a possibility in 1919.

Special Military Areas were created, such as one in Tipperary after the Soloheadbeg ambush, and these regulated public assemblies and movements. Of course, they were immediately interpreted as martial law under another name. When Limerick was proclaimed a Special Military Area in April 1919, local workers proclaimed a 'Limerick Soviet', i.e., a general strike. A committee took over Limerick city, imposed its own controls over goods and production, and created its own currency. As James Casey wrote in *Limerick's Fighting Story:*

The pickets ... paid particular attention to the opening and closing of shops at the prescribed hours, for the sale of necessary food, regulated queues outside provision shops, and controlled traffic. In fact, it was generally admitted that the city was never guarded or policed so well previously. The people for once were doing their own work, and doing it properly. Public houses were not allowed to open during the strike ... There was no looting, and not a single case came up for hearing at the Petty Sessions ... After nightfall, relays of boats with muffled oars were successfully used to run the food and other supplies through the blockade, and to maintain communication with the citizens. Numerous stratagems were employed to elude the military cordons, and funeral hearses from the Union Hospital and other districts outside the city did not always have a corpse in the coffin.

This 'Soviet' lasted only twelve days, but alarmed the government still further, even though the labour movement in Ireland had not supported the Limerick workers. The fear of 'Bolshevik' revolution was sweeping Europe, after the success of the October Revolution in Russia in 1917.

The next crisis was caused by the need for conscription. Most of the cabinet were against widening the net to include young Irishmen, as they sensed a growing lawlessness in the country. The RIC was weakening under relentless attack, and police were beginning to resign from this permanent, pensionable job, a clear sign of anxiety. The British army in Ireland was undermanned and consisted mainly of raw recruits. This is why the decision was finally made to draft non-police into the RIC, establishing the Black and Tans and the Auxiliaries. The RIC inspector general resisted strongly, realising the kind of men who were likely to come forward, but French won his point in the end. He insisted that the Irish were 'impulsive and quick-witted, but not a deep-thinking people', that they were being intimidated by Sinn Féin and the IRA, and that these organisations could easily be destroyed.

Recruitment poster for the Royal Irish Constabulary.

'I call it perfect madness,' she protested, 'to go down into the very thick of all those mad Kerry gunmen. I won't sleep a wink till you're back.'

'...My dear,' [said her husband], 'If you lived in Kerry and saw this kind of thing in the papers and believed it, would you think of coming to Dublin? Look here: "Ambush in City Thoroughfare. Heavy Casualties. Unknown man found dead at Drumcondra. Lively Exchange of shots in Dublin Bank. Suburban Mansion gutted." You'd think your life wouldn't be safe for a moment here, and yet it hardly worries us at all.'

FERGAL McGRATH SJ, *The Last Lap*, Dublin, 1925

Certainly, in 1919, there was still little sign of a central authority organising resistance to British rule. The war was a matter of individual attacks and skirmishes, seemingly on a random basis. Some attacks were properly planned, and looked for permission from IRA GHQ. One of these, in Fermoy, County Cork, was carried out by the North Cork Brigade on 7 September. Fifteen soldiers were attacked and their weapons seized, but one died, despite warnings to avoid killings. IRA GHQ was worried about the effect on local opinion if violence increased, and indeed British troops looted some shops in Fermoy in reprisal. No one was quite sure who the public would blame for this – the aggressions of the IRA, or the reprisals of the British army. However, once the coroner's jury in Fermoy described the killing as 'an act of war' and not murder, IRA GHQ sensed that the mood of the country was with them, and began to authorise more ambushes and raids.

The IRA men in the field were contemptuous of needing GHQ's permission for activities, and its constant requests for written reports which ran the risk of falling into enemy hands. Ernie O'Malley, Commander of the Second Southern Division, in particular complained that no one in GHQ ever came down south to see for themselves what was happening. In December, however, the Tipperary men were given a leading role in an attack on Lord French at the Phoenix Park, Dublin. Hand grenades were thrown at the convoy of cars, but French was not injured. One attacker died, and one detective injured himself by accident, but the attack shocked Britain, one newspaper stating the incident was 'elaborately planned

A flying column with Ernie O'Malley, probably back row, fourth from right, without a hat. Because of the covert nature of his work, this is one of the only known photographs of O'Malley from this time.

and carried out with remarkable daring and conviction'.

The following year, 1920, saw a huge increase in the number of RIC barracks attacked. A battalion of Cork No. 1 Brigade IRA attacked Carrigtwohill barracks. The garrison surrendered after explosives were used to blow down a wall. Shortly afterwards, sixty men attacked Kilmurry barracks; French asserted that these were 'acts of war'. A number of attacks in counties Longford, Wicklow, Monaghan, Cork and Kerry gave a sense of success to the IRA Volunteers, but there were more failures than successes. However, the effect of one RIC barracks being defeated would cause surrounding barracks to empty as well, leaving the countryside undefended.

RIC garrison, Kilmallock, County Limerick, 1920, photographed during the War of Independence.

About 11 pm, the soldiers returned to the town [Balla, County Mayo], attacked the police barracks, the walls of which are now bespattered with bullet marks, and also the windows of the chapel next door. After this reprisal on the police, they proceeded to shoot up the town, to break into houses and fire shots up through the ceilings, and to demand more drink. They then went to the convent on the outskirts, got over the wall and got into the keeper's lodge. They asked the man if he had any daughters, and hearing a young girl cry out, frightened by the noise, they burst into the bedroom where three girls, sixteen to twenty years, were in bed. One of the soldiers loaded a rifle and pointed it at the youngest, threatening to shoot her if she did not keep quiet. His comrade tried to disarm him and in the scuffle, while the soldiers fell over the bed, the girls in their night-dresses escaped from the house and fled to the convent for refuge.

ARMY OFFICER, 15 November 1920, quoted in Dorothy Macardle, *The Irish Republic*

To commemorate Easter Week, GHQ had the idea of burning three hundred police barracks simultaneously over one night, to great public effect. Four hundred barracks had been destroyed by July, and almost fifty courthouses. Income tax offices were also being burned down. There was still no overall plan of campaign for the IRA, and experienced officers were being very thinly stretched. O'Malley found that military discipline was hard to enforce; men expected guerrilla warfare to be fought without training or military techniques. They also underestimated the fighting abilities of the enemy, which operated under proper military discipline. Training in the use of weapons was time-consuming, and it was difficult to find out even how many weapons there were. Companies kept this information to themselves, afraid that the battalion commander would redistribute them.

The Cork commander, Tomás Mac Curtain, was trying hard to keep his men under control, but they chafed under the lack of orders from GHQ. The more militant among them began to attack police indiscriminately, without orders or plan; an off-duty constable was shot on 19 March, without Mac Curtain's consent. The pace of events grew swifter; in May, a barracks in Tipperary was attacked by O'Malley and others, climbing onto the roof with guns, grenades and a tin of petrol. They barely escaped burning themselves, and were finally driven off. Other attacks of this kind failed, but the pressure kept up.

Meanwhile, political events moved on. Local elections were held in January 1920. Sinn Féin had always had a strong tradition in local government. These elections had already been postponed more than once, and in 1919, proportional representation had been introduced for them. The British government hoped this would damage the Sinn Féin vote, but, in fact, Arthur Griffith had always wanted PR, and it was a Sinn Féin policy. The party now won the lions' share of the vote, and local government in the south and west of Ireland came under Sinn Féin control.

Cork and Limerick Corporations pledged to recognise Dáil Éireann as the government, which meant losing funding from the existing Local Government Board (LGB), a severe loss. Mac Curtain became mayor of Cork, but was shot dead in his home on 20 March, possibly by RIC members. He was replaced by Terence MacSwiney. When W.T. Cosgrave, Dáil minister for local government, was arrested, he was replaced by Kevin O'Higgins. Dublin recognised the authority of the Dáil on 3 May. In July, Britain issued an ultimatum, insisting on the authority of the LGB. This concentrated minds, and local authorities all over Ireland defied the ultimatum and accepted the authority of Dáil Éireann.

Rural elections, held in June, had copper-fastened Sinn Féin dominance. The party had produced policy documents on such matters as housing, health and education, and was looking more and more like a proper political party. However, the Volunteers still held the upper hand, and even picked the election candidates. Often these were wanted men, so local authority meetings were being held in unusual and secret places, guarded by Volunteers. Sinn Féin continued to publish *The Irish Bulletin* as its propaganda tool.

Appearing five times a week, it counteracted the British newspaper accounts of the war, referring to all British actions as 'aggression', and all republican actions as acts of war. In the *Bulletin*, the war was a matter of a sovereign state resisting an invasion.

A further indication of growing republican strength was the takeover of the justice system. 'Sinn Féin courts' were to be established around the country, and litigants were encouraged to use them instead of the British legal system. In May 1920, Austin Stack, minister for home affairs, published a scheme of arbitration courts, with a right of appeal to district courts. He intended this as only the start, before the entire legal structure could be replaced. By June 1920, it was reported that Sinn Féin courts were well established, but quite a few of these were military, set up for courts martial.

A serious problem for the courts system was an explosion of agrarian violence, not seen in Ireland since the previous century. Since the rule of law had collapsed with the retreat of the RIC, many long-buried land disputes were resurrected, and aggrieved tenants began to take the law into their own hands. Groups tried to seize grazing lands, to redistribute them, and the Dáil had to take direct action. Art O'Connor, minister for agriculture, set up a provisional land court in County Mayo. Its first case found against the claimants, who had been intimidating landowners, but the claimants refused to accept its decision. The local Volunteer commander was instructed to imprison them until they accepted the authority of the court, and he did so reluctantly, but it had the desired effect.

Gradually it became clear that the British legal system was no longer functioning in large areas of the country – although some litigants, unwilling to accept the decision of one court, would turn to the opposing system for justice. The success of the Sinn Féin courts made the Dáil look more and more like a functioning government. The collapse of the RIC's information system made it extremely difficult for the British administration or military forces to corner their opponents, and it became clear that enormous numbers of troops would be needed to control the country. As Britain was still recovering from the First World War, the prime minister, David Lloyd George, was reluctant to sanction this move, and very worried about what it would cost, in men and money.

MOVES TOWARDS PEACE

Home Rule had been passed in 1914 but postponed for the course of the First World War. In preparation for it, Britain passed the Government of Ireland Act in 1920, which was to create two parliaments, north and south. This would copper-fasten the existing partition of the island, and the powers of the two proposed parliaments were quite limited. There was provision for a Council of Ireland, if the two parliaments ever decided to unite; this would be almost dominion status and more than Ireland had been offered ever before. However, this outcome was extremely unlikely. The Ulster Unionist Council had finally agreed to a six-county state, with a voting majority of two to one. They lost counties Donegal, Cavan and Monaghan.

While these plans were being laid, Hamar Greenwood, chief

secretary in Dublin Castle, concentrated on restoring order. The head of the British Army in Ireland, General Sir Nevil Macready, was very reluctant to engage in a policy of coercion, feeling that it would only make bad worse. A prison hunger strike in April 1920 almost caused a crisis. The republican prisoners were demanding prisoner of war status, and by 9 April ninety men were on hunger strike. Crowds surrounded the prisons, barely held back by British soldiers, and public disorder grew. It was decided to release 'on parole' those men who were most at risk of death, but many others were released as well, by accident.

This was a propaganda victory for Sinn Féin, and it was supported in May by a labour strike, when dockers refused to handle cargo from Britain. When railway workers supported them, the railway companies sacked those workers involved, and the nation's rail network came to a standstill. Funds were raised for striking or sacked workers, and the IRA helped by transporting stranded passengers. Some of the workers alleged that they had been intimidated by the IRA to join the strike. By November, it was clear that the strikers were being starved out. There were not enough funds to sustain them, and in December they voted to return to work. Meanwhile, a Sinn Féin boycott of goods from the north, starting in August 1920, continued until 1921, along with a counter-boycott from the north.

Other violent events were swaying public opinion away from British rule. In September 1920 Kevin Barry, an 18-year-old student, was executed for his part in an attack on British soldiers, in which one was killed. His death provoked massive demonstrations.

It was followed in October by the death of Terence MacSwiney, after seventy-four days on hunger strike. He had been jailed in Cork for IRA activities, but was transferred to Brixton Prison when he refused food. More massive demonstrations of support for Sinn Féin took place.

I opened the window in the dark and sat down on the floor beside it. It was a wonderful still warm night and I could hear every sound from the town from where we were on the shores of Lough Atalia. The lorries full of armed men tore down the road from Renmore and the shooting began. The first shots sounded like a machine gun followed by a dreadful screaming. This was when Sergeant Fox shot young Séamus Quirke. Quirke was taken from his lodgings in the new dock and shot through the stomach eleven times. He crawled on his hands and knees from the lamppost on the quay where he was shot, to the door of his house. This screaming was the background to all the horrors of the next five hours until the poor boy died at dawn. Father Griffin was sent for and stayed with him till he died.

... The next thing was the sound of Johnny's mother, Mrs Broderick, screaming when they shut her in her house on Prospect Hill and set it on fire with petrol. The neighbours ran to put it out but were shot at and had to wait until the RIC went away again ... One after another the lorries went back to the barracks, leaving the RIC alone in the streets quite mad with blood. It was a planned outbreak of terror. While the RIC and Tans were doing all this, the Auxies were enjoying themselves working down a list of houses which were to be looted...

GERALDINE PLUNKETT DILLON, *All in the Blood*

Michael Collins's 'Squad' included, from left to right: Michael McDonnell, Tom Keogh, Vincent Byrne, Patrick Daly and James Slattery. Collins was president of the Supreme Council during the War of Independence, and this group of agents within his Special Intelligence Unit acted as his bodyguard. Led by Patrick Daly, they were also responsible for assassinations, including the murders of British intelligence agents on Bloody Sunday, 1921.

In October 1920, a number of Irish republicans were shot by British secret service agents. The agents had been active in the country for some time. Michael Collins was intent on destroying this nest of spies, using his counter-intelligence service, known as 'The Squad'. On Sunday, 21 November, fourteen British agents were shot dead by Collins's men. Retaliation was immediate: that afternoon a GAA match in Croke Park was interrupted by Black and Tans, who opened fire on both the players and the spectators. Twelve were shot dead and sixty wounded, some by the stampede that ensued. That night, three IRA prisoners were shot in Dublin Castle, apparently 'attempting to escape', but the wounds on their bodies told a different story. Matters were coming to a head, and both sides were running out of any option except an inexorable increase in violence.

Elections for the northern and southern parliaments were held in May 1921, and Sinn Féin candidates were elected in force. Instead of forming a Southern parliament, they called themselves the Second Dáil Éireann. When King George V opened the Parliament of Northern Ireland in Stormont House, Belfast, on 22 June 1921, he made an emotional speech calling for peace and reconciliation. Prime Minister Lloyd George followed this by approaching Dáil Éireann, and proposing a truce during which Ireland's future could be decided, peacefully.

Sinn Féin and the IRA were extremely surprised by this approach, because they had known they could not resist British military power if Westminster decided to throw more troops and money at the problem. But Lloyd George was not prepared to send in 100,000 men, at a cost of £100 million, as his army chiefs were telling him to do. Meanwhile, the activities of the Black and Tans and the Auxiliaries were upsetting public opinion in Britain, and the powerful Irish-American lobby was influencing United States opinion against British policy.

Members of the American Committee for Relief in Ireland inspecting the ruins of Balbriggan, County Dublin. The village had been destroyed in an attack by the Black and Tans in September, 1920.

Lloyd George gambled that if the Irish refused the truce offer they would be seen as unreasonable, and a tougher security policy would then be supported by the British public. Sinn Féin realised this, and also that Irish public opinion would be annoyed if the truce was refused. The population had endured some very difficult years, and was yearning for a peaceful solution. A truce was agreed, with the help of some influential southern unionists. Each side committed to stop all military activity, to stop collecting arms and supplies, and to avoid disturbing the peace. But the IRA looked at the truce as a temporary measure, during which they could replenish their strength.

The War of Independence had ended, with the prospect of what looked like more success than any previous rebellion in Ireland. The time had come for negotiation, with the hope of achieving a peaceful solution. The Irish plenipotentiaries set out for London in October 1921, but without their most prominent politician Éamon de Valera, by his own decision. The following weeks would lead to a new Anglo-Irish Treaty, and precipitate a short, but damaging, civil war.

PICTURE CREDITS

The author and publisher would like to thank the following individuals and institutions for their permission to reproduce images.

National Library of Ireland: pages 14, 16, 17, 24, 30, 33, 38, 41, 44, 53, 59, 60, 70, 74, 82, 84, 85, 86, 113, 128, 154, 155, 163 and 173. National Museum of Ireland: pages 94, 98, 100, 104, 106, 108 and 114. *History Ireland*: pages 99 and 161. Kilmainham Gaol Archives: pages 119, 143 and 150. Glucksman Library, University of Limerick: pages 127 and 133. Royal College of Surgeons in Ireland: page 143. Mercier Press Archive: pages 164 and 171. The O'Sullivan Family: page 151. Commemorative plaque of Anne Devlin, courtesy of the author; designed by Y. Drori; produced by Irish Celtic Art Studio, Monaghan, Ireland; photo by Emma Byrne: page 63. The following images were scanned from books in the author's personal library. John Mitchel, *Jail Journal*: pages 77, 78 and 80. *Voice of Ireland*: pages 120, 122, 124, 130, 137 and 153. E. Roper, *Prison Letters of Countess Markievicz*: page 148.

SUGGESTED READING

1798

Bardon, Jonathan. *A History of Ulster*. Belfast: Blackstaff Press, 1992.

Dickson, D. et al. (eds.). *The United Irishmen: Republicanism, Radicalism and Rebellion*. Dublin: Lilliput Press, 1993.

Dunne, Tom. *Rebellions: Memoir, Memory and 1798*. Dublin: Lilliput Press, 2004.

Gahan, Daniel. *The People's Rising, Wexford 1798*. Dublin: Gill & Macmillan, 1995.

Killen, John (ed.). *The Decade of the United Irishmen: Contemporary Accounts, 1791–1801*. Belfast: Blackstaff Press, 1997.

MacDermot, Frank. *Theobald Wolfe Tone*. London: Macmillan, 1939; republished Dublin: Anvil Books, 1968.

Murphy, J.A. (ed.). *The French Are in the Bay: The Expedition to Bantry Bay, 1796*. Cork: Mercier Press, 1997.

Pakenham, Thomas. *The Year of Liberty*. London: Hodder & Stoughton, 1969.

Stewart, A.T.Q. *The Summer Soldiers: The 1798 Rebellion in Antrim and Down*. Belfast: Blackstaff Press, 1995.

1803

Finegan, J. (ed.). *Anne Devlin Patriot & Heroine: her own story of her association with Robert Emmet and her sufferings in Kilmainham Jail.* Dublin: Elo Publications, 1992.

Geoghegan, Patrick M. *Robert Emmet: A Life*. Dublin: Gill & Macmillan, 2002.

Hume, G. and A. Malcolmson. *Robert Emmet: The Insurrection of 1803*. Belfast: 1976.

McDowell, R.B. (ed.). *Memoirs of Miles Byrne*, Shannon: Irish University Press, 1972.

1848

Gwynn, Denis. *Young Ireland*. Cork: 1948

Mitchel, John. *Jail Journal: With an Introductory Narrative of Transactions in Ireland*. Dublin: M.H. Gill, 1921.

Moody, T.W. *Thomas Davis, 1814-45: A Centenary Address Delivered in Trinity College, Dublin, on 12 June 1945 at a Public Meeting of the College Historical Society.* Dublin: Hodges Figgis & Co., 1945.

1850s–1880s

Comerford, R.V. *The Fenians in Context: Irish Politics and Society, 1848–82*. Dublin: Wolfhound Press, 1985.

Golway, Terry. *Irish Rebel, John Devoy and America's Fight for Ireland's Freedom*. New York, 1955; Dublin: Irish Academic Press, 1998.

Kenna, Shane. *Jeremiah O'Donovan Rossa: Unrepentant Fenian*. Kildare: Irish Academic Press, 2015.

Kenna, Shane. *War in the Shadows: The Irish-American Fenians who bombed Victorian Britain*. Kildare: Irish Academic Press, 2014.

McGee, Owen. *The IRB: The Irish Republican Brotherhood from the Land League to Sinn Féin*. Dublin: Four Courts Press, 2005.

Rose, Paul. *The Manchester Martyrs: A Fenian Tragedy*. London: Lawrence & Wishart, 1970.

Ryan, Mark. *Fenian Memories*. Dublin: Gill, 1945.

1916

Clarke, Kathleen. *Revolutionary Woman*. Dublin: The O'Brien Press, 1991; new ed. 2008.

Collins, Lorcan. *1916: The Rising Handbook*. Dublin: The O'Brien Press, 2016.

Duffy, Joe. *Children of the Rising: The Untold Story of the Young Lives Lost During Easter 1916*. Dublin: Hachette Books Ireland, 2015.

Foy, M.T. and Barton, B. *The Easter Rising*. Stroud: The History

Press, 1999.

Gillis, Liz. *Women of the Irish Revolution*. Cork: Mercier Press, 2014.

McCarthy, Cal. *Cumann na mBan and the Irish Revolution*. Cork: Mercier Press, 2007.

McCoole, Sinéad. *Easter Widows*. Dublin: Doubleday Ireland, 2014.

MacEntee, Seán. *Episode at Easter*. Dublin: Gill, 1966.

McHugh, Roger (ed.). *Dublin 1916*. London: Arlington Books, 1966.

Plunkett Dillon, Geraldine. *All in the Blood: A Memoir of the Plunkett Family, the 1916 Rising and the War of Independence*. Dublin: A&A Farmar, 2006.

Pyle, Hilary (ed.), *Cesca's Diary, 1913–1916: Where Art and Nationalism Meet*. Dublin: Woodfield Press, 2005.

Taillon, Ruth. *How History Was Made: The Women of 1916*. Belfast: Beyond the Pale, 1996.

Townshend, Charles. *Easter 1916: The Irish Rebellion*. London: Penguin, 2005.

Readers are also directed to the series, *16 Lives*, first published by The O'Brien Press in 2016, which consists of biographies of the sixteen men executed after the Easter Rising.

1919–1921

Casey, James. *Limerick's Fighting Story*. Cork: Mercier Press, 2009.

Foxton, David. *Revolutionary Lawyers: Sinn Féin and Crown Courts in Ireland and Britain, 1916–1923*. Dublin: Four Courts Press, 2008.

Griffiths, K. and T.E. O'Grady. *Curious Journey: Oral History of Ireland's Unfinished Revolution*. London: Hutchinson, 1982.

Townshend, Charles. *The Republic: The Fight for Irish Independence*. London: Penguin, 2013.

Ward, Margaret. *In Their Own Voice: Women and Irish Nationalism*. Dublin: Attic Press, 1995.

GENERAL WORKS

Boyce, D. *Nationalism in Ireland*. Dublin: Gill & Macmillan, 1982.

Boyce, D. (ed.). *The Revolution in Ireland, 1879–1923*. London: Palgrave Macmillan, 1988.

Conlon, Lil. *Cumann na mBan and the Women of Ireland, 1913–25*. Kilkenny: 1969.

Costello, Peter. *The Heart Grown Brutal: The Irish Revolution in Literature, 1891–1939*. Dublin: Gill & Macmillan, 1977.

Foster, Roy. *Vivid Faces: The Revolutionary Generation in Ireland, 1890–1923*. London: Penguin, 2014.

Garvin, Tom. *The Evolution of Irish Nationalist Politics*. Dublin: Gill & Macmillan, 1981.

Kee, Robert. *The Green Flag: A History of Irish Nationalism*. London: Weidenfeld & Nicholson, 1972.

Laffan, Michael. *The Resurrection of Ireland: The Sinn Féin Party,*

1916–1923. Cambridge: Cambridge University Press, 1999.

Macardle, Dorothy. *The Irish Republic*. Dublin: The Irish Press, 1937.

Maguire, Martin. *The Civil Service and the Revolution in Ireland, 1912–38: 'Shaking the Bloodstained Hand of Mr Collins'*. Manchester: Manchester University Press, 2008.

Matthews, Ann. *Renegades: Irish Republican Women, 1900–1922*. Cork: Mercier Press, 2010.

Maume, Patrick. *The Long Gestation: Irish Nationalist Life, 1891–1918*. Dublin: Gill & Macmillan, 2000.

Moody, T.W. (ed.). *Nationality and the Pursuit of National Independence*. Belfast: The Appletree Press, 1978.

O'Halloran, Clare. *Partition and the Limits of Irish Nationalism*. Dublin: Gill & Macmillan, 1987.

Phoenix, Eamon. *Northern Nationalism: Nationalist Politics, Partition and the Catholic Minority in Northern Ireland, 1890–1940*. Belfast: Ulster Historical Foundation, 1994.

Vaughan, W.E. (ed.). *A New History of Ireland V: Ireland Under the Union I, 1801–70*. Oxford: Oxford University Press, 1989.

Vaughan, W.E. (ed.). *A New History of Ireland VI: Ireland Under the Union II, 1870–1921*. Oxford: Oxford University Press, 1996.

Ward, Margaret. *Unmanageable Revolutionaries: Women and Irish Nationalism*. London and Kerry: Pluto Press, 1983.

Zimmerman, G.-D. *Songs of Irish Rebellion: Political Street Ballads and Rebel Songs, 1780–1900*. Dublin: Allen Figgis, 1967.

INDEX

KATHLEEN CLARKE
Revolutionary Woman

Edited by Helen Litton

Only first person account of 1916 ever published

Illustrated with rare historical material and photos

A compelling and genuine first-hand account of an activist during the most exciting and turbulent period of Irish history, Kathleen's story is one of incredible personal courage and commitment. Documenting the setting up of Cumann na mBan, the O'Donovan Rossa funeral, Kathleen's time in prison with Countess Markievicz and Maud Gonne MacBride, it also covers the Black and Tan raids, the Treaty, the Civil War, and Kathleen's time as Dublin's first female Lord Mayor and gives us a unique female perspective on these events.

THE 16LIVES SERIES

• Biographies of the 16 men executed for their role in the 1916 Rising
• Meticulously researched
• Written in an accessible fashion

JAMES CONNOLLY LORCAN COLLINS

MICHAEL MALLIN BRIAN HUGHES

JOSEPH PLUNKETT
HONOR O BROLCHAIN

EDWARD DALY HELEN LITTON

SEÁN HEUSTON JOHN GIBNEY

ROGER CASEMENT ANGUS MITCHELL

SEÁN MACDIARMADA BRIAN FEENEY

THOMAS CLARKE HELEN LITTON

ÉAMONN CEANNT MARY GALLAGHER

THOMAS MACDONAGH SHANE KENNA

WILLIE PEARSE RÓISÍN NÍ GHAIRBHÍ

CON COLBERT JOHN O'CALLAGHAN

JOHN MACBRIDE DONAL FALLON

MICHAEL O'HANRAHAN
CONOR KOSTICK

THOMAS KENT MEDA RYAN

PATRICK PEARSE RUÁN O'DONNELL

ABOUT THE AUTHOR

Helen Litton is the author of six illustrated history books, and of two volumes in The O'Brien Press Sixteen Lives series, *Edward Daly* and *Thomas Clarke*. She is the editor of *Revolutionary Woman*, the autobiography of Kathleen Clarke. Helen is married, with two children and two grandchildren, and lives in Dublin.